SCOTLAND

The Land and the People

Donald Cowie

SOUTH BRUNSWICK AND NEW YORK:
A. S. BARNES AND COMPANY
LONDON: THOMAS YOSELOFF LTD

© 1973 by A. S. Barnes & Co., Inc.

A. S. Barnes & Co., Inc.
Cranbury, N. J. 08512

Thomas Yoseloff Ltd
108 New Bond Street
London W1Y OQX, England

Library of Congress Cataloging in Publication Data

Cowie, Donald.
    Scotland: the land and the people.

    1. Scotland—Description and travel—1951–
I. Title.
DA867.C68 1973   914.1   72-6383
ISBN 0-498-01169-0

Photographs supplied by courtesy of The British Tourist Authority, London

PRINTED IN THE UNITED STATES OF AMERICA

for

THOMAS YOSELOFF

(with grateful thanks for making it possible)

CONTENTS

SCOTLAND

1

THEN AND NOW

SCOTLAND is one of those countries which should not exist, being barren mountains largely under pluvious skies. Four out of the five millions of miniature population crowd together for warmth in a narrow plain between the firths of Clyde and Forth. Throughout history it has been repeatedly invaded, and knew peace only when finally conquered by the English.

It has some quaint customs and a certain life of its own but has become little more than an appendage of England. The British Empire started there; and still the remotest hamlet of the farthermost Highlands must ask London's permission before it digs a sewer. England collects the taxes and many Scotsmen can be excused for wondering if they get back as much as they pay.

It would be nice if one could say at once that Scotland in compensation has contributed more to civilization than many other nations. It would be pleasant to compare her with other miniscule countries, like Greece, Holland, Switzerland, even Israel, who have maintained independence against heavy odds and at the same time shaken the world with their arts and ideas. Alas, this pleasure is not possible.

Why not?

The answers in a stale age will come not from recapitulation of the old myths and popular ideas but only from a journey which avoids most of the trodden ways. It will be necessary to turn up the coat collar and march off valiantly into the mist, forgetting about the jokes and bagpipes and coach tours, conquering our modern world-weariness by taking the wrong turning on every possible occasion and refusing to be attracted by an out-of-date holiday plan.

This world-weariness is not just Scotland's disability. It is responsible for the way our children behave everywhere in spite of

A photograph cannot usually reveal the full interest of Princes Street, Edinburgh, one of the most beautiful city streets of the world. This photographer has nearly succeeded. The Scott Monument is in the foreground.

our inordinate kindness to them. It explains why wealthy retired people go mad amid their pleasures and why craftsmen no longer take much trouble over their work. It is the age not just of disillusionment but of the sickness that overtakes a man when he has done it once too often.

So Scotland could, by a real cynic, be completely written off. Once upon a time it was a picturesque appendage to England, and its children were amusing because they worked so hard and tried to be so clever, and, above all, were so worried when they lost money. Edinburgh had excellent hotels and other facilities such as palatial tearooms and shops selling silver and shortbread and tartans and tweeds. Maybe the English royal family (of Scottish origin of course) was at Balmoral Castle and there was a monster in Loch Ness. Abbotsford still remained as Sir Walter Scott had left it, a magnificent memorial to supreme authorship and bankruptcy combined.

It was possible to leave King's Cross railroad depot in London of a honey-colored July morning amid florid and weedy individuals in tweed breeches surmounted by Norfolk jackets, whose quiet and Derby-hatted servants put shotguns and fishing tackle in the luggage compartment. The talk would all be of hooking salmon on the river Spey and of the prospects for grouse when the shooting season officially opened on the "glorious" August 12th. One would join house parties in ancient, crenellated houses with as many as fifty bedrooms,

This is Britain's highest mountain, Ben Nevis (4,406 feet) with Fort William beneath.

an equivalent quota of staff, and perhaps an odd bathroom or two tucked away at the cold end of one of the mile-long passages.

The golfer could go to St. Andrew's where the Royal and Ancient was the most important course in the entire world or he could enjoy himself with an old iron for no more than half a buck on any of a hundred seaside and municipal links amid lemon-sanded dunes outside "unspoilt" towns of sad grey stone and highly risible natives.

There were Highland Games where immense men tossed young pine trees called cabers (from the Gaelic word "cabar," a pole); and uproarious "Burns nichts," or banquets devoted to the memory of the national poet Robert Burns, which were preluded by the ceremonial arrival of musicians in Scottish fancy dress whose function was to "pipe in the haggis" (a sheep's stomach boiled after filling with minced guts and lungs, mixed with onion, oatmeal, suet, pepper and salt).

Glasgow was not just the third largest city in Britain. It was also one of the world's greatest industrial centers and in particular the place where nearly all the great ships were beautifully built, ships that were sold to America and Russia, New Zealand and South Africa, Hong Kong and Brazil.

The world's linoleum came from Kirkcaldy and its jam from Dundee. The trawlers and drifters off the north-east coast provided Europe with various kinds of pickled and smoked herring. Women in every country sewed with Scottish cotton. It was impossible to wear a cardigan or pullover without paying financial tribute to a cluster of hard-working small towns in the Scottish lowlands such as Hawick and Galashiels.

We went to Scotland not only for a pure brand of different pleasure but also for good business. It was an international workshop, second only in the British Isles to that extraordinary city called Manchester.

And wherever a Scotsman went in the world he was welcomed. This was partly the product of his brains and skills. He was outstandingly good at the construction and maintenance of machinery and at the tending of gardens and young children. He possessed in addition a degree of financial ability that had been equalled in history only by the Lombards and by the Jews. The greatest corporations of London and the United States and China and New Zealand were in the executive control of either Scots or Israelites.

Our modern world was made by such as Rockefeller but also by such as Andrew Carnegie, the poor boy from Dunfermline in Scotland, who created not only Pittsburgh and most of its industries but also that world-shattering institution, the free public library.

But the Scotsman was welcomed all over the world not just for his technical and financial abilities. He was actually liked everywhere; and there is to this day probably no nationality that is better worth boasting about than Scottish. Maybe this is in part due to the corresponding aversion felt towards many Englishmen. The English kept to themselves, formed their own societies, even permitted others to know that England was a superior country. Or they were always more embarrassed when brought into unwilling contact with fellow men, and so got that reputation for being cold and distant. (Perhaps they were just a little more cagey and wary than other, less-civilized peoples!)

How Scottish golf began (and continues) the course being at remote Boat of Garten, Inverness-shire.

The Scotsman by contrast was so friendly and open, so warm and unaffected. He possessed the chameleon-like quality of being able to adjust himself to any environment. His outstanding skill was to be able to do in Rome as the Romans did. The typical Scot, successful and deservedly popular, had blue eyes and red-gold hair, lived in many countries and developed as many different clothing and speech habits to taste. In an international gathering he would quick-change his parts just like a character actor.

So Scotland had and has a good press. It was like the Kennedy type of politician whose smile wins him votes wherever he goes (and no matter what he does).

It was a good place with an excellent reputation, and its only real shame was its essential poverty, derived, of course, from its misfortunes. (The cogency of that will be analyzed later).

Then it could produce an Admirable Crichton and a Walter Scott, not to mention a Bobbie Burns; and it could build the world's finest ships.

But its death rate, its infant mortality rate, and its susceptibility to the tuberculosis germ were among the highest in the world; and it was not for nothing that its slender population was steadily denuded by wholesale immigration to other, less demanding lands.

Scotland today is not what it was partly because nothing is anymore what it was anywhere. But there are other, less general reasons why the greatness and the charm have so tragically departed.

Therefore to seek the best of that country now, and to enjoy not only a sojourn there but also an account of its history and achievements, it will be necessary to avoid the accustomed ways and to go mainly where the guide books consist of blanks. We are finished with what meant so much to our forefathers; and our future pleasures will mostly lie where formerly there were none.

2

ENTRANCE

S COTLAND, of course, has one of the finest airports in Britain, at Prestwick in Ayrshire, notable chiefly for size of runways and comparative freedom from the fog that can close down London. But small countries like Scotland and Holland like to boast of such assets. They need to. It is an exhibition of their essential inferiority complex. Everything in Scotland must be best to the vanquished Scot, everything from the strawberries to the ships to the books to the football to the number of awards for gallantry won by her sons in foreign wars.

So many must fly directly from Kennedy to Prestwick. It is inadvisable but it is often sensible and necessary. And it certainly has the advantage of inoculating the wary at once against a kind of madness which has been profitably erected into a major industry by this Old World.

The visitor who arrives at Prestwick will be tempted, nay, often forced by the terms of his tour, to explore the "Burns country" which is one of the appendages of the airport. There are the souvenir kiosks, the untidy restaurants, the hotels, and the "Burns country."

This consists of a rolling agricultural region, not unlike parts of New England, falling one side to a rocky sea with a strange and mountainous island in the middle, and rising on the other side to windswept, sheep-cropped hills. There are a few grey towns and many hamlets of low white hovels, and a great deal of nice, clean-looking cattle, the famous Ayrshires.

Robert Burns was an unhappy young man who lived before his time in the eighteenth century. He would have been much happier today, with a beard and hair to his shoulders and a fine pattern of heroin shots on his right arm. Only he would not have bothered to write the poetry if he lived today. There would have been no need to. Generous money would have been given to him as a layabout by the State and his dreams would have been enjoyed silently during trips on a pad.

In the eighteenth century he could get only whisky and women and these were not enough, so, as a hard-working farmer's bad son, he had to write down his fantasies and try to get them published. Then he would perhaps make some mark in society and get some money to pay for the whisky and women. It was a strange society, that of the eighteenth century, one where there were crude roisterers on this side and would-be aristocrats who paid at least lip-service to learning and culture on that.

After his father's death young Burns became tenant with his brother of a farm at Mossgiel. Instead of working hard and helping his brother properly, he ran after the girls day and night in intervals of drinking himself silly, and he tried to write some of that poetry. He did it in the same way as a young man today would try to get on television. It was one of the easiest eighteenth century ways to fame and fortune.

The first poems that the roisterer wrote, in plain English, were far too bad to be acceptable even in a bad century. The plainness of the English exposed the banality of the thought and the inability of the mind to soar. But then Burns had the brilliant idea of joining those who, for hundreds of years in Scotland, had made money out of the old songs handed down.

Primitive man was extraordinarily fortunate in that he had no books. So he had no so-called civilization. But he had to amuse himself in the evenings, and so arose the ancient race of bards, people who were too weak or cowardly to hunt and fight and bought their bones by singing the praises of those who were strong. Poetry, music, the dance and the theatre all started thus.

Scotland has always been one of the richest countries in the world as regards folk ballads, for three good reasons. First, she remained comparatively uncivilized for much longer than most white countries. Second, she lost most of her wars and was crushed by conquerors, than which there is no more effective recipe for the concoction of sad old songs. Third, she quite chancefully evolved a series of pseudo-scholars who learnt how to make a good thing out of listening to the folklore and folk music and writing it down.

By the time Burns wanted a way of getting into print there were many collections of songs and epic poems in the Doric (local dialect or rough speech, a name derived from what they called the talk of peasants in ancient Greece).

The Birthplace cottage of Robert Burns at Alloway, Ayrshire, typical of the earlier domestic architecture of the region.

So Burns one day had his inspiration and took one of the old songs and polished it a little, improved its prosody. The result, when he read it out to friends in a tavern, was uproarious.

So he tried again, and again, and eventually he took off from the ground on his own and he soared.

There is no doubt that Burns at his best is one of the world's greatest lyric poets or literary songsters; also that Shakespeare even at his worst is the world's greatest dramatic poet; and it is interesting to note that both got away from the ground only on the shoulders of former writers. As Burns initially got his impetus from the old folk ballads of his locality, so Shakespeare lifted the plots of his plays unashamedly from piles of old play sheets used at the Globe Theatre where he worked in London.

Burns was little more than a peasant and a very bad one at that. He helped to ruin every farm on which he worked. But he possessed this knack for re-writing a folk song and turning it into high lyric poetry, a knack that became gradually something more than that when he turned to incidents of his own everyday life and wrote them down in the crude local speech:—

> O saw ye bonnie Lesley
>   As she gaed o'er the Border?
> She's gane, like Alexander,
>   To spread her conquests further.

That is the original clodhopper Burns, re-writing the time-old songs of his district. But:—

> Of a' the airts the wind can blaw,
>   I dearly like the west,
> For there the bonnie lassie lives,
>   The lassie I lo'e best:

And:

> O my Luve's like a red, red rose
>   That's newly sprung in June:
> O my Luve's like the melodie
>   That's sweetly play'd in tune!

> As fair art thou, my bonnie lass,
>   So deep in luve am I:
> And I will luve thee still, my dear,
>   Till a' the seas gang dry:

Those are the authentic notes of the wild bird singing, and no matter the circumstances. No matter that he was trying to get around Jean Armour, the good girl, while callously playing the horses of the innumerable others like the buck stallion he was. It was simple stuff, involving none of the profound thought or the rich word-magic of a Shakespeare. But it was great lyric poetry, made out of local dung; and to this day there is nothing else like it anywhere, if one excepts the too-brief excursion of Edward FitzGerald into the similar folk-lore of old Persia (and perhaps some of the wanderings of a still underrated Edgar Allan Poe).

Burns enjoyed a considerable literary success with the first volume of his verses, entitled *Poems, chiefly in the Scottish dialect*, which was published in Edinburgh in 1786 thanks to the kind patronage of a local tycoon. (What the world and literature owes to the generosity of maligned rich men!) Second and third editions in subsequent years gave the young man sufficient meagre means to enable him to marry the difficult Jean and start farming on his own account down south near Dumfries. The success also won him a useful part-time sinecure as a revenue officer. Two years later the fool drunk and wenched himself out of the farm, and was rewarded suitably with a full-time revenue job. But he could not last. He was torn apart by the demands of his crude nature on the one side and the divine poetry in him on the other. He fornicated and drank himself into the inevitable ditch of his death, at the perfect poetical age of thirty-five.

Nothing could be more alien to the favorite Scottish mentality than Burns. The Scottish values are hard work, learning, careful control of lusts and appetites. The Scots are like the Swiss and the early New Englanders and the orthodox Israelites who wrote the Old Testament in that they believe above all things in clean living and rigid self-control. Not far away from this "Burns country" of Ayrshire had rigidly ranted and preached the ineffable apostle of Scottish Calvinism called John Knox. His doctrines of hell-fire and damnation for all who dared to dance on Sundays seized the imagination of the Scottish people far more than all the fairer philosophies of the globe.

Yet the Scots rapidly made the poor poet and doomed rake Burns into a national hero; and in this Lowland part of the country, Ayrshire and around, they permitted their commercial sense to create the madness against which the visitor has already been warned. Ayr itself, near to the great airport, has the "Tam o'Shanter Inn," after one of Burns' roistering friends. Alloway, not so far away, contains the sacred shrine of the birthplace cottage, a redecorated hovel with the inevitable turnstile and the poet's books and scraps of correspondence and pieces of glass upon which he had written with a diamond. (Until comparatively recently this was a strange preoccupation of genius; and without a doubt diamonds used to be a poet's best friends).

Kilmarnock, amid its drab and tottering manufactories, has a Burns Monument and Museum; and the minute place of Kirkoswald contains riches indeed, not only "Souter Johnnie's" House—"Souter" was another Burns character—but also the churchyard graves of the local louts whom the poet immortalized as such and as "Tam o'Shanter."

Dumfries down south is in the Burns business almost as efficiently as Pittsburgh is in steel. There are not only the Burns House, with more relics of the man's daily life, but also, supreme irony, his pew in St. Michael's Church. A visitor deliciously imagines what stirrings there must be in the nearby grave as he is reverently shown the seat where the good Christian once worshipped. And there are a Burns Walk and at least two Burns taverns, the Globe and the Hole I'the Wa'. These are rather more authentic.

Not far away the great writer business extends to no less a crashing bore than Thomas Carlyle, whose birthplace at Ecclefechan is tended as the shrine it must be to any Scotsman who appreciates what can quickly turn a buck.

One of the better aspects of a Scottish town of the Lowlands: that Ayr where Robert Burns once roistered.

There are several more places, back in Ayrshire, where the gapers can continue to gawk. Mauchline, for example, contains a Burns House with museum, and there is a hideous Burns Memorial Tower, and the local graveyard features the graves not only of local characters he made famous but also of four of his several children. (How many Scots must be descended today from those hedgerow couplings!)

Tarbolton, not far away, is where Burns foregathered often with men friends in intervals of making women out of local girls such as that intriguing Mary Campbell, the "Highland Mary" of the poems. She worked as a dairymaid at the Castle o'Montgomery, on high ground above Tarbolton.

But it is a madness of the past, this commercialization of the places where miserable writers and artists once comported themselves; and it no longer works in an age when we are too wise to be amused any longer.

If the transatlantic visitor arrive by jet at Prestwick today he can inoculate himself against further attacks on his commonsense by briefly touring this typical "Burns Country." The desire to see further hollow shrines should be out of his blood after that.

Really the best way into Scotland is from England, because then the immediate difference between the two countries can be more properly appreciated.

There are few borders in the world more typically to be seen as frontiers between different cultures.

This is because the Scots and the English are completely different from each other, and because the border area is, for the British Isles, quite vast and mountainous.

The difference between the Scots and English will gradually be explained in this book, but immediately even the most obtuse visitor will note that the English of Northumberland and Cumberland, the border counties, speak like the Scots but are bigger and stronger and infinitely more placid. They are somehow dull; and it is understandable that for hundreds of years they were the prey to Scottish marauding bands, whose national sport then was not football but riding hell-for-leather into England at night and making off with cattle, sheep and women (in that order, of course).

The placid English would do comparatively nothing till their government in London spoke, and then an army would efficiently march up into Scotland and, defeating the bandits in pitched battle, quiet them for a few months at least.

Scotland used to begin at Hadrian's Wall, some hundred miles of rough stone fortification, built by Hadrian, one of the best of the ancient Roman Emperors, between the years A.D. 122–6 for the purpose of keeping the wild Picts and Scots at bay. This wall was originally the outermost limit of the civilized world and beyond it lay only the deep space and wildness of what we now know as Scotland.

There are two great main roads, from Carlisle north to Glasgow and Edinburgh, and from Newcastle north to Edinburgh (plus a modern motorway), but they have been worn into such familiar tracks that a wise man would always avoid them these days (unless indeed he be a motorized salesman) and would best come into what remains of the real Scotland after spending a night in the nice little Angel Inn at Corbridge not far from the Wall. Next morning the car mounts a narrow and up-and-down but surprisingly straight hill road with a minimum of fellow traffic. Under the smooth surface are undoubtedly the solid stones of an original Roman road.

The skies lift and distances spread and larks rise twittering to the empyrean and in season there is golden gorse that pops when the bleak sun comes out.

These Cheviot Hills straddle the border between Scotland and England and are not only unnaturally vast for such a small country—all a matter of relativity—but they still give in an overcrowded and polluted period of history a feeling of wildness and wonder and solitude. The curlew cries and a solitary truck might be dangerously negotiating the Kalahari Desert. Little villages seem to be precariously temporary settlements of impudent, pioneering man. Only the sheep-clipped and tawny grass everywhere makes these different from the mountains of the moon.

This enormous area of the counties called Roxburgh, Berwick, Selkirk and Peebles has industries that have been mentioned already, notably concerned with the fabrication of local wool into knitwear and tweeds. These have tended to price themselves out of real prosperity in recent times thanks to teaching their tricks to the Italians of Milan and the Chinese of Hong Kong, and the Japanese, and even the English of Leicestershire. But the Cheviot Hills of the Border really remain what they have always been, a comparatively vast area of bleak upland pasturage for the limited production of some unique races of sheep, cattle and men.

The indigenous men have never been numerous. Food and climate have seen to that. Like the mountain Swiss, they have been whittled away by the environment as a stick is whittled, to a whiteness and bleakness of pure form. They have long heads and firm mouths and chins, and their eyes have the keen look of shepherds searching in a snowstorm for sheep. Most of them have at sometime or other searched in a snowstorm for sheep.

These sheep have helped to provide the world with its wool and mutton in modern times. They created Australia and New Zealand, and they extend across the United States, Canada and South America, nibble delicately in Japan, and are now being imported increasingly into Soviet Russia and China. The principal breeds, such as the Cheviot, the common Blackfaced, and the Border Leicester, have no equal among the sheep of the world for hardiness, productivity, and above all the quality of transmitting characteristics undefiled to subsequent generations.

There was, for example, a farm at Clackmae, just off this central Edinburgh road near Earlston; and the proprietor, keen and shepherd-eyed, was a direct descendant of no less a typical Border country man than James Hogg. (The very name "Hogg" was once pseudonymous with "sheep.")

Coming just after James Burns, this Hogg was known in the romantic early nineteenth century as "The Ettrick Shepherd." Until thirty years of age he could neither read nor write. This advantage helped him a lot later on when he began to write poetry. He taught himself (which is really the only way and a sad commentary on the millions we devote to schools). In intervals of tending sheep—perhaps an hour in the evening and a stolen hour or two on Sundays—he made himself a more cultivated man than nearly everybody in the highly "civilized" world of today.

And the verses that this "Ettrick Shepherd" wrote, how wonderful they are! Maybe they never soar to the pure heights of Robert Burns' poetry, but they are often expressed in better English, as the famous *Boy's Song*:—

> Where the pools are bright and deep,
> Where the grey trout lies asleep,
> Up the river and over the lea,
> That's the way for Billy and me. . .
>
> Why the boys should drive away
> Little sweet maidens from the play,
> Or love to banter and fight so well,
> That's the thing I never could tell.
>
> But this I know, I love to play
> Through the meadow, among the hay;
> Up the water and over the lea,
> That's the way for Billy and me.

Burns could sing better than anybody, and interpret the everyday life of the peasant perfectly, but he could never write so purely in

English as the less favored Hogg, nor could he attain Hogg's extraordinary vision as expressed in the long poem *Kilmeny*. The girl
Kilmeny is spirited away to another world and returns. What she
saw in that other world was identical with the experiences of all the
great visionaries. Maybe she was indeed teleported to the true place
of our origin. The gentle, homespun "Ettrick Shepherd" had that
superb idea nearly two centuries ago. And it is very great poetry:—

> She saw a lady sit on a throne,
> The fairest that ever the sun shone on!
> A lion lick'd her hand of milk,
> And she held him in a leish of silk;
>
> And a leifu' maiden stood at her knee,
> With a silver wand and melting e'e;
> Her sovereign shield till love stole in,
> And poison'd all the fount within.

The Hoggs still farm to this day in the country where their ancestor was a shepherd of genius; and they look like him and they
produce wonderful cattle and sheep, of the sort that can be exported
at high prices to all sensible parts of the world.

The secret hereabouts is continuity. The men produce animals that
breed true and they breed true themselves.

Another sign on the central Edinburgh road, but farther south than
Earlston, points to Ancrum. There is a fine old estate known as
Kirklands. When this was visited only a few years ago the owner was
a descendant of the Scotts of Buccleuch, a tall man of formidable
presence. He had been bred exactly in the mould of his ancestors
who controlled this entire Border area by a combination of strong right
arms and superior minds, and now he was devoting the same skill to
the scientific breeding of Hereford cattle. Upon rich green pastures
under red cliffs. ('Tis the sandstone that counts!)

Contemporaneous with Hogg was another of this remarkable, ruling
family of Scotts, that Sir Walter whose literary career was the exact
opposite of Burns's and a far more typically Scottish achievement.

The night now should be spent at Kelso, which is nicely off the
beaten tracks and contains an excellent hotel, Ednam House, that
overlooks the fast-running River Tweed, and contains scales in the
entrance hall for weighing the fly-fisherman's salmon after he brings
home the catch. People stand about both in the Tweed and in tweeds,
and gaily-colored artificial flies decorate their Sherlock Holmes hats.
Hands are always being spread about, not in expostulation, but in
measurement.

To walk about Kelso of an autumn evening after a couple of malt whiskies in the bar of Ednam House is to learn a lot about the differences between Scotland and England. This town, like all in Scotland, is completely foreign in appearance. It strangely resembles a small town in provincial France, even to the type of signs over the shops. It is severe and logical by comparison with the often picturesque muddle of an old English town. The center is a wide place paved with the flat stones of Europe. The old houses rise high and the people live in them in apartments. Maybe there are no concierges but there should be.

Throughout its history Scotland was nearer to France politically than to England. "The Auld Alliance" is still there in the minds of the people and the architectural outlines of the towns. Marxists would explain this in terms of capitalistic pressures: Scotland had to trade with Europe as England deliberately squeezed her into poverty. But the animal breeder would probably be more accurate when he pointed instead to racial origins.

The original inhabitants of modern Scotland were the same "Celts" from north of Greece who overran and created France. Some of these stuck in England but not enough.

It will, however, be shown in a later, historical section of this book, how those "Celts" possessed every virtue and vice save the ability to fight large-scale wars successfully.

So the percipient visitor knows at once in Kelso that the surroundings and spirit of the place are more like France than England: and he observes equally how there is this pervading sadness in the landscape, the architecture, the poetry and the songs. It is a sensation of failure.

Even the great Scott failed. He was born in Edinburgh in 1771, the son of a lawyer, and he qualified as an advocate himself, but suffered infantile paralysis long before Salk and was thereafter left with a limp and a fierce desire to prevail over affliction. And that is the true Scottish desire.

He significantly married a wife of French origin and he learnt German to translate old ballads and this gave him a similar idea to that of his contemporary Burns.

Only it must be understood at once that Walter Scott was not a heavensent poet and disgraceful rake like Burns. He wrote volumes of so-called poetry that is really just rhyming prose, and then he wrote a long series of historical novels. All was good work for that time, and the English prose of the Scotsman was often excellent, but never, never world-shaking.

The kind of architecture Scotland produced in the best of her early days: Traquair House in Peebles-shire of the Lowlands.

Robert Burns had more influence with a single line—"A man's a man for a' that"—than Walter Scott had with his millions of admirable but basically turgid words.

First of all Scott collected local ballads and published them in his *Minstrelsy of the Scottish Border* (1802). Then he wrote his long narrative poems, based largely on those earlier researches, poems such as *Marmion, The Lady of the Lake, The Lord of the Isles.* These chiefly celebrated the martial achievements of the military asristocracy from which his own family had sprung.

It was a period, the early nineteenth century, when easily-read verse could be easily sold, and Scott rapidly made a small fortune from his poems, or at least a small fortune for those days.

With this money, what did he do? He began to build a baronial house at Abbotsford on the River Tweed up above Kelso and near the delectable ruins of Melrose Abbey. This he did slowly, putting money into the great house pound by pound, until eventually it was one of the most remarkable pieces of pastiche in the British Isles, that is to say, a romantic, nineteenth century re-creation of a state of splendor that never was or had been. To this day it can be visited and wondered at, even deplored, but never truly despised. It represents in bricks and mortar what has always been the secret spiritual ambition of western man, to be the big man.

There at Abbotsford the lame Edinburgh boy gradually became a national figure and a baronet. He was granted this temporal nobility by his English King in 1820. He walked about his extensive estate with a shepherd's crook and a favorite dog; and grateful tenants doffed their bonnets to him as the laird. He was a good landlord, and the marks of his improvements on the formerly poverty-stricken district are still there. And he still brings money to the district in the form of tourist tolls.

But he did not have quite enough money from his poems to complete the building of the great house with its turrets and crenellations and sharp-pointed Gothic windows of expensive stained glass. So he turned, at first secretly, to the writing of a would-be popular prose romance. He was so ashamed of venturing into this low field that he refused to put his name to the eventual publication of *Waverley*.

The enormous success of that novel—rather incomprehensible today—eventually persuaded the careful man to sign his name to the long series of further romances, *Guy Mannering, The Antiquary, Old Mortality, Rob Roy, The Heart of Midlothian, The Bride of Lammermoor, Ivanhoe, Kenilworth, Peveril of the Peak, The Talisman, The Fair Maid of Perth*. It was a prodigious production, probably unequalled in literary history and typically Scottish, because these were not slender modern novels but infinitely-long, infinitely-detailed historical recapitulations, quite perfectly done if practically unreadable to all save the bravest today. One such novel in his entire life would be enough for any modern author to write (after which he would probably suffer a mental breakdown).

Actually Walter Scott did suffer a mental breakdown, but not because he wrote so hard. It was because he had put the money not needed for Abbotsford into a firm of Edinburgh printers and publishers called Ballantyne and Company, who had associated themselves with the famous publisher Constable—and Constable went bankrupt. One day—the year was 1826—poor Scott learnt that the combined debts of these firms with which he was financially associated were some four hundred thousand dollars, which, in those days, was big money, equal perhaps to several million today.

Now the true Scot in Scott came right up to the surface. He took coach into Edinburgh and informed his white-faced partners there that he had no intention of taking advantage of the bankruptcy laws. He would himself, personally, pay off the debts.

This he very nearly did before he died, and soon after his death in 1832 the last debts were actually paid off on the security of his copyrights.

They were six years of the hardest literary work ever performed by a human being. Scott wrote from morning to night and never gave himself a chance. He wrote for money and he wrote increasingly badly—*Woodstock*, a life of Napoleon, *Tales of a Grandfather, Count Robert of Paris, Castle Dangerous*, many others—but he kept his promise and paid off those debts.

Therefore Scott continues to live in Scotland and in many parts of the world not so much as a writer as a man. His is the similar fame of a mountaineer or a Francis Chichester.

It is also very like the fame of Samuel Johnson in that it might never have been appreciated but for the work of a literary parasite of genius, in Scott's case J. G. Lockhart, his son-in-law, who in 1837 published a life of the great man which is still one of the greatest biographies ever written. Two Lowland Scots, Boswell and Lockhart: they are still unbeatable as writers of biography, and perhaps only Lytton Strachey may sometimes be admitted to the same unique class.

In the olden days these Lowland Scots were organized in gangs by fierce marauding types who behaved very much like medieval Al Capones. The gang leaders were mostly of Norman origin, descendants of Scandinavian sea rovers. They had come to Scotland either across the North Sea, red-bearded in long-boats, or as part of William the Conqueror's entourage from Normandy, France, in 1066. They had no difficulty in organizing the essentially money-loving Lowland peasants for cattle rustling forays into England and for a favorite sport they invented, blackmail. This was a method of obtaining regular contributions by threats which was later to be copied on a grander scale by the Mafia in Sicily, by the street boys in Chicago and New York, and by charitable organizations everywhere.

A fearsome man named Douglas was the most considerable of these

gangsters, and his career and that of his descendants frequently for
centuries afterwards, was an object lesson to all who despair of our
rough world's future. The Douglases time after time again paid the
full price of their sins. They suffered even more than those they had
wronged, right down to Lord Alfred Douglas, the beautiful boy and
excellent poet who over-excited Oscar Wilde.

And the same good law of nature, ensuring that the wicked robber
barons should completely exterminate themselves eventually, handed
back the homespun Scottish Lowlands in the eighteenth century to
representatives of the original indigenous inhabitants for control. This
is, therefore, the part of the British Isles which in modern times has
contributed most to the sobriety of the British reputation.

James Boswell, the Lowland Scottish biographer of Dr. Johnson,
was typical of the breed. He was essentially a second-class man as
a man, a prey to venereal disease but not so openly that you would
mark it, and in his literary work he was so unadventurous that naturally
he became a biographer of genius. Unlike Walter Scott he did not
have to strain after worldly success. His ancestors had been the lords
of an estate called Auchinleck for generations. He just wrote soberly,
perfectly for the purpose, and kept the dirty part of his life carefully
out of sight of the neighbors' eyes.

John Buchan was another typical product of the modern Lowlands,
the sort of quiet young man who would never stand out in a crowd,
but possessed of a bulging intellect, an infinite capacity for hard work,
and of course that essential provincial skill in masking the lower
regions of manhood. He could be a best-selling writer of thrillers, a
superb popular historian and biographer, a fine soldier, a reliable politician and an excellent administrator. The only thing he was not was
a poet and man of destiny. His fate was to become Governor-General
of Canada and the first Lord Tweedsmuir.

Another very typical Lowland Scot of the modern type was Douglas
Haig. Towards the end of the First World War young Britons tended
to regard him not only as one of the most handsome of military men
but also as the supreme military genius on the Allied side. He was
the victor of that war and received the immediate rewards of an earl-
dom and some 400,000 dollars, also a decoration called the Order of
Merit which is named thus because it is given by the monarch in
Britain to those who seldom merit it.

During the 1920s there occurred in Britain the final flowering of
an age-old literary tradition. It was fragile, irreverent work, typified
by the writings of Lawrence, Huxley, Norman Douglas, Strachey.
Influenced by the spirit of these final men were young military com-

mentators like Liddell Hart; and very soon these were probing into the reputation of Douglas Haig.

They found that his famous offensive battles of the Somme, July-November 1916, and Passchendaele, July-November 1917, were among the most costly in all military history. Passchendaele was the culminating martial flower. British casualties alone were some 400,000 men, including no fewer than 17,000 gallant young officers.

So Haig was revealed with his feet of clay and for a long time was execrated.

Then we had another war and a new generation arose which had no personal experience of the first, and slowly Haig came back. It was seen that he represented the dogged British spirit at its most unbeatable. Without him the British at least might have lost on the field of battle to the Germans and the American intervention might have come too late. Moreover it was seen that only Haig's influence upon the French supreme commander Foch made possible the 1918 attack towards the north which finally broke the Hindenburg Line and sent the Germans running for home and Hitler.

So Haig finally made it. He represented the sober, indomitable courage of the Lowland Scots (even though his name also represented a famous whisky).

It is possible, of course, that yet another generation might swing back and ask why Haig was not shrewd like Julius Caesar, a military commander who made rather than destroyed an empire by never, never bashing away at hopeless frontal attacks but always finding a devious and surprising way round.

Britain at this time of writing still has a typical Lowland Scot high in its counsels. He is Douglas-Home, one of the human powers behind Edward Heath. Like all Scottish politicians he is clever, hard working and liked even when laughed at, in his case for his aristocratic blood which, in an over-democratic age, has barred him from the highest power. Also he possesses the rather typical Scottish inability to look really convincing as well as beautiful on television.

3
EDINBURGH AND GLASGOW

SCOTLAND has two real cities, Edinburgh and Glasgow, and they are about as different as any two cities could be. Edinburgh is beautiful. Glasgow is ugly. Edinburgh is the proud, historic capital. Glasgow is larger but industrial and was in its day the workshop of the world. Edinburgh has culture so thick that not even Boston could equal it. Glasgow is rough and common. If you reeled into Edinburgh belching they would pull the drapes and leave you alone in the broad, bleak street. Your same behaviour in Glasgow might introduce you to several uproarious parties at once. There is rather a similar contrast in Australia, as between the pride of Melbourne and the raucousness of Sydney. Probably the wise man finds good in both, although sometimes it is difficult.

The beauty of Edinburgh proceeds from its geographical features and its architecture. The geographical features comprise several strange hills, like those of Rome, and then a rapid descent to the broad sea water of the Firth of Forth, above which arise the lemon-misted uplands of the Kingdom of Fife.

The architecture of the city is accidentally superb. Individual pieces, such as the pinnacled memorial to Sir Walter Scott in main Princes Street, can even be ugly on their own, but as part of the composition they are fine. Upon a hill to the left is the Castle, founded by Edwin of Northumbria, an English invader who gave Edinburgh its name. So even the Scottishness of Edinburgh is phoney. The next hill is that of Arthur's Seat. Who was Arthur? Surely not another damned and legendary Sassenach? Swing round again and there is a hill which is magnificently surmounted by classical columns and a plinth. Part of Athens, or where the Romans left their Scottish mark?

Edinburgh's Castle, one of the most famous in the world, but typically founded by an English king over 1300 years ago.

No, it is a comparatively modern memorial to a dead historical event, which the Edinburgh people left unfinished because so many of them wisely turned away when asked to contribute that first essential of the civilized life, money.

Princes Street, Edinburgh, was so often described by Scots as the finest street in all the world that inevitably they had to do their very utmost to destroy its beauty. In the nineteenth century they filled a strange canyon which runs alongside it with a railway and depots and smoke. In our own time they have replaced many of the lovelier Princes Street shops with the cheaper kind of chain stores, so that the names you see are often the same as those which make the main streets of suburban London such a familiar sight to those who arrive wondering from Tuscaloosa, Alabama.

And yet Princes Street remains indefinably exciting and beautiful. This is because the spectator can often see the thoroughfare as a whole, from a distance on high. Inevitably he mounts one of the pimple hills and looks down. Through the archane coalfire smoke— which long ago earned Edinburgh its endearing name of "Auld

*The old town of Edinburgh has many such nooks and corners as this
Bakehouse Close.*

Reekie"—he sees a long and wonderful street of shops and spires. The
gardens and trees on the left descend to the magic of the railway
gully. And on the right, dimly, is a stone wilderness of potentially
interesting architecture, the New Town.

*One of Scotland's greatest prides is Princes Street, Edinburgh, with the re-
markable monument on the left to her most voluminous writer, Walter Scott.*

First of all, let us briefly examine this phenomenon of masking
smoke. Do the anti-pollution people realize what they are doing?
They are trying, if fortunately without complete success, to strip away
the masking clouds of dust and carbon that, throughout long centuries,
have brought beauty and romance to otherwise dull townscapes.
Edinburgh is the outstanding example of what can be done with dirt
in the air, and of course London was a good second.

The man who mounts Arthur's Seat in Edinburgh and gazes down
is faced with an awful cauldron of mystery. If he were a painter he
would become a bigger and better J. M. W. Turner. The mystery is

caused by the wreathing smoke and atmospheric filth. This masks the squalor of the tall tenements and the gingerbread cheapness of the widespread ecclesiastical architecture.

If ever they succeed in eliminating coal and gasoline smoke from this town then it will abruptly cease to attract wondering visitors, who will see the place for what it is, a masterpiece mainly of mass production real estate development, rather like a bleaker Philadelphia on stilts.

The effect will be the same as in an expensive restaurant where there were once candles and soft music but now only bright ceiling lights and a military band. It will be like what happens to a woman, naked and without make-up in the full light of day.

Would life be worth living if we didn't smother it with sauces?

Secondly, let us move away from the chiarascuro and essentially false charm of the old tourist Edinburgh, and briefly examine that New Town.

This was originally a great residential district, descending towards the Firth of Forth; and they started to build it in 1767. It became one of the best monuments we have to the classical architectural renaissance of the eighteenth century, ranking with Bath and Dublin in this respect. And, strangely enough, it was created in an essentially indigenous style, proceeding from the poetic fantasies and monetary ambitions of local Scots, particularly the remarkable Adam brothers.

There were four of them, Robert, John, James and William, and they all became architects and interior decorators (one of them a useful banker also). The greatest was Robert, and he was probably responsible for what became the New Town style. He traveled as a young man in Italy and Dalmatia and made sketches of the Roman remains there. He came back and was appointed Architect to the British King and brought his brothers down from Edinburgh to help him with the rebuilding of a whole district in central London which became suitably known as the Adelphi (from the Greek for "brothers").

What the Adams did was design houses and their interiors in what they thought must have been the ancient Roman fashion.

Supposing New York is almost completely destroyed in atomic war, and, some seventeen hundred years later a descendant of Australian aborigines observes the few skeletonal ruins remaining of an Empire State building here and a United Nations building there and returns to the heart of his southern continent to build a whole city of what he imagines are twentieth century skyscrapers. The result would be amazing, but of course it would not be New York.

Thus the Adelphi, and then the New Town of Edinburgh, and

A typical tourist attraction in Edinburgh's old town, known as Greyfriars Bobby.

eventually pseudo-classical edifices right across the world, were essentially the expression of the brothers Adam's idea of how eighteenth century Britons might be able to live in the Roman manner. Actually it was just get-rich-quick jerry-building with classical orders stuck on.

But it was a damned sight better than most of the buildings that had been erected in London and Edinburgh before. The rooms were more spacious and the facades were more regular. And it was infinitely better than anything which followed, either in Scotland or California.

The interior streets of the New Town have long since been given over to shops and offices. George Street and Charlotte Square are no longer occupied by douce Edinburgh burghers trying to pretend they are ancient Roman senators. But the outlying and descending thoroughfares of the region remain sleepily as they were built. A visitor who carefully traversed them on foot would acquire in a few hours more knowledge of the past than he would get from weeks of gaping at Holyrood House and the Royal Mile and the Castle.

He would be well advised to continue his perambulations still further into the interminable suburbs of this great sprawling town, especially back through the smoke and out to such as Morningside, where the gardens and the front doors and the knockers are kept in such good condition that it is almost frightening. The very doorsteps are newly painted or holystoned. The occasional human being is so inhuman as to be instantly terrifying. The mouth is pursed and the eyes are icily cool. Not a hair is out of position and the clothes might be perfect representations of fashions that were favored by our fathers and mothers but, all the same, have obviously just been to the dry cleaners.

Another view of Edinburgh's Princes Street, this time with the emphasis on the Adam-type building of the Royal Scottish Academy.

A magnificent entrance gateway to the Palace of Holyrood House, Edinburgh.

This is the real Edinburgh, the real Scotland, and it is what has made possible the enormous contribution of the Scots to our material civilization. Banking and insurance, engines and gardens, and at least an effort to behave a little better than alley cats in social and sexual life: Scots from these douce suburbs, by their self-discipline and mutual repression, have—or did until recently—helped to make us better materially and keep us out of the primeval slime.

But cracks will already be seen. It is tragic. Up in the Royal Mile, that dark thoroughfare of the pseudo-historic, is John Knox's House, and John Knox, of course, was the sixteenth century religious reformer.

A less grandiloquent but homelier aspect of the real Princes Street, Edinburgh.

Young Scotland at work, learning to be surveyors in Edinburgh, and displaying the sartorial prosperity they have gained from the union with England (also the kind of architecture that has been imposed upon them).

Modern architecture in Scotland: the Arts Block and Library of the University of Edinburgh.

He was not only the Calvin of the north but also a fine writer of Scottish prose. His style was as bleak as the religion he preached and if he'd had his way no one anywhere would have had any kind of fun ever. It was just sinful and if you didn't eschew the pleasures of life you would be damned.

Another less grandiloquent aspect of Princes Street, Edinburgh.

This icebound man did so well from his preaching that in his late middle-age he dressed like a prince and furnished his house like a lord and wore expensive jewelry and fine clothes. And at the age of fifty-nine he married a girl of seventeen.

There are those even in our present permissive age who would call him a dirty old man.

Similarly the douce suburbs of Edinburgh today are not all inhabited by inhuman perfectionists. Quite a lot of their sons and daughters are dirty and untidy and like to sit on paper-strewn pavements outside the concert halls wherein are held pop festivals as presided over by hairy drug-takers from the cosier pads of San Francisco.

Only the sociologically inclined should linger around the high Castle of Edinburgh or the palace known as Holyrood House at the other end of the Royal Mile. The true history has departed long since from the entire area just in the same way as much of the furniture and other trappings have gone from the cold palace rooms. The area is half municipalized. That is to say it has been stripped and tidied and is presided over by government custodians in uniforms like cops. It has the same atmosphere as a harlot in prison clothes. For the rest there are shops of souvenirs and so-called antiques and even places

*How Edinburgh looks from the Castle on a fine day: towards Princes Street,
the New Town, the Forth, and the hills of Fife.*

How the modern Edinburgh commuter lives.

where the antiques are made. And the blatantly false is best avoided by those who do not wish to suffer intolerable boredom at high expense.

Just occasionally the shopkeepers in these parts are or have been interesting because they themselves are or have been genuine. There was a woman who ran an antiques business in the Canongate and like John Knox she took to herself at an advanced age a much younger consort. If a client did not immediately buy from her she would tell him to get to hell out of it.

The Grassmarket is a broad enclave down a hill nearby, and in the good old days it knew constant riots and public executions. Now all is swept clean and the stones no longer stink of blood, but, in a genuinely-old shop are clocks of many kinds, and weapons, and armor; and Americans especially will remember with real affection "Mac" and his wife, he a stout, jolly man, ruptured awfully by youthful coal-heaving, infinitely skilled as a mechanic of timepieces, she a dark, intense woman who would detect poetry the instant it appeared, and would discuss mutual ailments or the universe for hours on end.

Oh, Edinburgh has these occasional pleasant surprises, but on the whole is no longer in existence as it once was.

The streetcars no longer rumble, nor do the bloody-handed nobles intrigue around their young and nubile Queen; the soldiery mostly lie rotting in some corner of a foreign field that is for ever England; the shortbread and the butterscotch and that once-delectable candy known as Edinburgh rock are packaged beautifully but that is about all. And even the great investment trusts are not exactly what they were. They are not any longer immutable.

Scotland has gone soft and bad like every other institution at the end of an era.

There was a young man descended from the earliest Scottish kings, titled, wealthy, inevitably educated in England. He took his guest into the Club on Princes Street and was extremely happy when the guest elected to drink only draught beer. His father, a belted Earl, controlled one of the largest Scottish ship-building yards and the family was connected also with great textile industries. The belted Earl sat in his castle with a shawl around his thin shoulders because he preferred not to waste money on a fire and of course central heating was out of the question.

The young man described how his wife had been injured in a road accident soon after marriage and how it had been impossible to obtain redress from the other offending motorist because, a gangster, he had been neither licensed nor insured.

Then the young man went on to recount his experiences as a part-

Golf for the people, on the Edinburgh Municipal Course, with "Auld Reekie" in the background.

time magistrate. He seemed to agree with the system of placing most criminals "on probation."

His ancestors would have had such criminals publicly executed after, probably, a prolonged session of torturing. They would not have been in any way better than their descendant save in their capacity for building a nation and giving it the proud, romantic name and the pride which Scotland once had.

Scotland is waisted at its middle and Glasgow is at the west end with Edinburgh at the east. This is a strange exception to the rule

Edinburgh workers go home from one of their most modern industries, that of Ferranti Electronics.

that west ends are best ends, socially at least. But it confirms the other rule that east is east and west is west and never the twain shall meet. There is as much difference between a Glasgow and an Edinburgh man as between a Hottentot and an Eskimo.

Glasgow at the end of the nineteenth century was among the most important industrial cities of the world. It was right at the top in shipbuilding and had some of the most prolific iron and steel foundries and engineering works ever devised by man. It lived for work alone and most of its inhabitants were so shrewd that they insisted on keeping a hand in their money pocket even when embracing their mothers. They grudgingly gave some money for the erection of dreary Victorian-type museums, art galleries, churches and colleges, but allowed their vast city to grow without conscious plan or nice embellishment. It became a dirty, aesthetic horror and no one would think of going there but for business or a helping hand in time of trouble.

Yes, the grim and hard-working Glasgow temperament was always mitigated by humanity (which may perhaps enable the city to survive when Edinburgh has been completely forgotten). This was partly due to the racial mixture, but also to the soft and humid climate as influenced by the Gulf Stream drift. Glasgow men quickly became intoxicated and excitable. And sentimental. Their favorite local songs were those which expressed their real love for a dirty, untidy, uproarious old town.

A visit to Glasgow, then, while not strictly advisable, would certainly teach the trained observer a lot about the Industrial Revolution, its architecture and its social effects. And, of course, about what has gone wrong with Britain since.

James Watt, the true founder of our modern mechanized society, was born in 1736 at Greenock, then a fishing village at the mouth of the Firth of Clyde, a few miles west of where Glasgow now sprawls.

The father of this all-important man was not a low laborer but a merchant and magistrate. Romance is nearly always wrong. Nor was young James Watt an infant prodigy. He was a sickly child and suitably annoyed his parents because he took every opportunity to stay home from school and avoid the other children. All he did was read books and cover paper with useless mathematical calculations.

The upright and successful father can be imagined talking to the purseproud and worried mother: "He has just this single talent, which he has obviously inherited from his grandfather and my brother, who as you know are at least good engineers and clever at figures. But he would never succeed at college, so I suggest we put him to work at once. I have been told of this instrument maker in London who is willing to take apprentices."

The boy was put on a horse-drawn coach, which eventually reached London; and there he spent just one teenage year, learning how to cut brass and make the instruments then employed by university mathematicians, chemists and engineers for their calculations. It was fine, accurate work; and the instruments were the first real machines of our modern industrial age. Such instruments, together with time-pieces and the crude apparatuses of flour mills, laid the foundations of our mechanical civilization, although they were by far the most important of the three types. James Watt's boyhood work in the eighteenth century was that age's equivalent of working with advanced electronic computers today.

The London climate proved to be even worse for young Watt's lungs than seaside Greenock's had been. After that single year he came whining home, much to his parents' disgust. After that he just mooned around for a year or two, but gradually obtained jobs of work, notably in the sparetime manufacture and repairing of violins.

When he was twenty-one years of age Watt heard that the University of Glasgow wanted a full-time maker of mathematical instruments for its infant laboratories. He applied for the job and he got it. The reasons for this success were that he was one of the few people in Scotland who had some knowledge of how to make mathematical instruments—and that the pay was so small that only a rich man's son could afford to take it.

The world owes a lot to James Watt's indulgent parents. They gave the young man just enough to keep him from completely starving, and in due course he was forced to use his brains hard to make a little more money. All day long for ten years he endured the monotony of making the same simple instruments for the use of students and researchers at the University. Then in the evenings he began gradually to experiment. Thus he invented the micrometer.

The primitive instrument of Watt's devising might not mean much to the modern reader, and it certainly meant less than nothing to most of his contemporaries. But Watt's original micrometer was the first instrument ever for making very small measurements with the greatest accuracy. Without it, and its many children, modern engineering could never have developed. There would never have been a washing machine nor would we ever have reached the moon.

Modern Scotland: a Civic Centre at Motherwell and Wishaw, just outside Glasgow.

That was pretty good for a sickly, half-starved and constantly despised young man in the murky Scotland of the eighteenth century.

Soon after he had reached thirty years of age James Watt began to blossom, in two ways. First, he started to receive some minor commissions in what amounted to civil engineering, connected with projects such as harbors and canals. Probably he owed this to the family influence of his uncle the engineer.

Second, he became interested in the infant steam engine.

At the University of Glasgow was a model of the original precursor of the modern piston engine, Newcomen's atmospheric pump. It had been devised for the purpose of extracting water from flooded mines. It had many defects, and the University's model, being almost unworkable, was handed over to young Watt for repairs.

For two years Watt experimented with the engine, probably secretly. And, early in his investigations, he found that most of the energy generated by the crude machine was wasted. He determined to discover how this fatal defect could be eliminated. And his eventual solution involved the application of an entirely new principle in motive power.

Instead of allowing condensation of steam to operate the piston in the cylinder, as Newcomen had clumsily contrived, Watt constructed a separate condenser, closed the cylinder top and bottom, and connected the piston with a beam. The idea was for the piston to move the separate beam upwards and downwards. Then Watt made by hand brass valves for admitting steam alternately above and below the piston. Not only was this principle sound but it worked splendidly. Not only was the steam engine invented, but also the principle of the modern internal combustion engine had been discovered. When Watt was making that crude machine with his own hands he was also making the modern automobile and aircraft industries.

Of course the young man himself could never have foreseen the great changes that would be brought about in the world by the agency of this first childish steam engine. In the middle of the eighteenth century, when Watt was at work, all industry was the product of hand labor. Horse-drawn and wind-powered mills did little to eliminate the activities of human hands, arms and legs. Thousands of possible industrial processes could not be put into being because of lack of power.

Any survey of the history of what is called the industrial revolution will show that most of the great changes of that epoch—the sudden increase in population and the development of dark, satanic mills in which textiles, metalwares, footwear and ceramics were produced on a large scale quickly—date approximately from the time when

Britain decided universally to use James Watt's steam engine.

He experienced some difficulty at first in putting it over, but obtained general assistance much quicker than is the rule with such epoch-making discoveries. Perhaps the law of averages was compensating him for his earlier disappointments and privations. If you don't get it at one end of your life you get it at the other (provided you have done the necessary work).

Watt's real stroke of luck was his encounter, through the instrument-making side of his work, with a Birmingham engineer named

At the heart of Glasgow, in typical weather, is the strange 19th. century beauty of City Chambers, St. George's Square.

Matthew Boulton, a rich but still enterprising man who had inherited a silversmith's business.

This Boulton deserves lasting fame not only because he helped James Watt launch the steam engine as a practical proposition, but also for many other achievements, including the production of some of the best early Sheffield plate—and the very best English ormolu ever made. (Much of this work, which has great interest for the expert in antiques, was done to the designs of another Scotsman, the aforementioned classical revivalist, Robert Adam).

Anyway Watt and Boulton got together and in 1773 they patented and offered for general sale, the steam engine.

And, almost at once, the industrial world eagerly took to the marvellous, original machine. Mine owners, cotton spinners and weavers, manufacturers of woollen textiles, iron founders—they expensively installed new and successive editions of Watt's engine as quickly as they could be built.

This was all extremely good for Watt. Nothing succeeds like excess. A little politician is a radiant, big man once he becomes President. So our sickly poor Scotsman developed into a strong and long-lived celebrity. He lived to the fine age of eighty-three—and he never ceased to work.

Much of his time was devoted to continually improving the steam engine. In the years 1781, 1782, 1784 and 1785 he notably obtained patents for such as the expansive principle, the double engine, the parallel motion and the smokeless furnace: most of which assisted the task of using steam pressure for the propulsion of machinery in mills. His final steam invention of genius was the governor, using a watchmaker's principle for the control of the awful energy that a steam engine could produce.

He devoted the rest of his time to general research and to continual self-education. Some biographers claim that Watt was the original discoverer of the composition of water. Others note that he and Boulton developed the coin-making machine which produced the coinages of the nineteenth century. And the old man actually earned the numerous honorary degrees he was given by universities by dint of beating everyone in general knowledge. He became so well-read and his memory remained so prodigious that in a more fortunate age he would have won all the jackpots on the quiz programs.

When he died at Heathfield near his Birmingham works on August 25, 1819, he was nationally mourned as the great man he had always been.

Another typical Glasgow man and contemporary of James Watt's was that Adam Smith who was the virtual founder of modern economics. During his years as Professor of Moral Philosophy at the University of Glasgow—he had been born in Fife but lived his real life in Glasgow—he gradually worked up the theories finally to be published in his *An Inquiry into the Nature and Causes of the Wealth of Nations*.

Out of this dirty and striving Glasgow had come the steam engine and thus the industrial revolution. Adam Smith devised a philosophy to explain away the revolution. Thus it must always be. A practical man invents the wheel and the priests soon start prating of Zoroaster. Adam Smith's insistence upon the basic importance of labor and the necessity of freedom to trade not only nationally but also internationally was responsible for several British and world developments. His teachings led to the deliberate creation of the British Empire across seas controlled by the Royal Navy as an outlet for British factory products, but they also inspired men to create and to yield to trades unions and undoubtedly they gave Karl Marx the basic ideas—reading away in the British Museum—for *Das Kapital* and so were responsible for the eventual Communist Revolution, which was to become no less potent when suffered bloodlessly in Britain and America and other western lands than it was when imposed by force in Russia and China.

During the great nineteenth century many lesser Glaswegians than Watt and Smith invented machines and processes and then explained away their purposes in windy words. The city grew like a cancer upon the formerly lovely land and it made money that manured not only the farflung lands of the Empire but also (let it be said softly) the former colony that was now known as the United States of America.

Glasgow literally worked itself to death in order to supply the world with ships and other goods and to make money for itself in the process, and when it grew tired towards the end, it turned as old men often do to teaching its skills to others. Just after the Second World War a cheap Glasgow hotel in Kelvingrove was filled with young Japanese. They said that they had come to Glasgow to study the methods of shipbuilding. Twenty years later Glasgow was losing most of the worthwhile shipbuilding contracts to Japan—and this was not due to the fact that she no longer had men of the calibre of James Watt to keep her ahead technically. It was primarily due to the fact that her blathering philosophers of labor like Adam Smith had convinced her working population that they were the aristocrats and why should they work anyway. The ships just could not be delivered on time anymore because the men preferred to dispute and take holidays rather than to work. (And when they were delivered, far too expensively, those ships, because of the disputes during their making, were dangerously defective.)

No single great writer ever came out of Glasgow, if one were to except the platitudinous imitation philosophers like Adam Smith and various theologians. The nearest to genius was perhaps that singularly unhappy and unfortunate man George Douglas Brown. He died in 1902 at the early age of thirty-three, a year after the publication, under the pseudonym George Douglas, of his remarkable little novel

How Glasgow tries to keep up-to-date—with modern cranes for loading rail containers on road vehicles.

The House With the Green Shutters.

Brown was a typical journalist of our times, the talented man who eventually drinks himself insensible because his sensitive soul cannot stand what he sees around him. But in *The House With the Green Shutters* he succeeded for once in sublimating his hatred of what Glasgow humanity had become. The novel is a merciless but stimulating exposure of greed and stupidity and of the dead end into which the urban Scots got themselves after a nineteenth century of working with the wrong values.

Needless to say George Douglas Brown is scarcely known in Glasgow today and few works on English literature spare so much as a sentence for his novel.

But a publisher who reissued it today might well make his second fortune from it, especially in television rights.

Completely to understand what made Glasgow tick in its heyday, however, it is necessary to read the best novel of that typical modern Scotsman John Buchan, whose career has been described before. This novel is *Huntingtower*. It takes a middle-aged Glasgow grocer out of his stolid, everyday life into a series of adventures up and down misty hills and crouching in the heather while villainous adversaries patrol the skylines and remorselessly advance like beaters. He enjoys these thrills side by side with a group of dead-end kids who call themselves the "Gorbals Die-Hards." And they are better companions and fighters than the best-trained soldiery from West Point.

The Gorbals is just the most notorious of several overcrowded districts in which the failures of Glasgow live. After Watt invented the steam engine people crowded in from the rural areas to get better money and more exciting conditions of life as factory workers. The money, these conditions and cheap food from the North American and other colonial countries enabled them to multiply rapidly. But it was bad, promiscuous breeding and did not improve the race of these originally sturdy countrymen. Glasgow soon became embarrassed with a surplus of increasingly inferior human beings. They were not clever or strong enough to succeed in the new industrial jungle, nor had they the courage and enterprise to get out quick and find better opportunities elsewhere. It was these unfortunate misfits who made the enormous and almost unique Glasgow slums.

The Gorbals is the perfectly-named archetype of all Victorian human garbage dumps. It consists of tall tenement buildings, wherein each single-room apartment will accommodate often more than one large family. As originally built in the nineteenth century these had primitive but adequate facilities for sanitation, cooking and heating, but even the best of the landlords could not maintain the buildings and their appointments in good condition or ever modernize them. They were not allowed by law to raise rents adequately and the tenants had absolutely no idea (at that period) of helping themselves.

Eventually, when it was too late, these dregs of humanity were gradually given better conditions with the help of money taken in taxation.

Yet the Gorbals, and many similar social plague-spots of Glasgow, were not and are not wholly garbage. The canyons of the rain-slimed streets would be filled at night with noisome mist and the odors of rotting people, but also with flitting gangs of boys and men, who were knife-fighters all.

Out of these gangs came some of the bravest and most desperate combatants of the two World Wars, as well as many of the most militantly successful of not only British but also American trades union leaders.

Also the Glasgow slums produced a majority of kind-hearted human beings, the kind who would succour a stranger or share a last crust

*More of the rail containers that help to answer Scotland's modern prob-
lems. These are at Grangemouth Docks.*

with a hated neighbor.

The workings of natural law seem to produce biological good continually from biological evil. Slums like the Gorbals were festering
diseases upon the land but occasionally a newly-hard and resistant
strain of bacteria would emerge.

The way the social and economic redemption of the Gorbals came
too late was this. It came from outside political action and the money
of stranger taxpayers, but it came when the breed of human beings
in the Gorbals was no longer any good for aught but desperate fighting and some remarkable acts of charity between the fights. The
people had become the misfits of an industrial society. They could
fight each other and be kind to each other but not work properly
any more.

This does not mean that they had necessarily lost their intelligence
or even their skills. It means they were no longer either houseproud
or capable of the continual, disinterested labor which is the only kind
that counts. They had found certain weapons which could cure their
misery, notably the strike, and work became just one more of the four-
letter words. (Probably it always had been with their particular families, which was the reason why they got into and created these
Gorbals in the first place).

It is too sad to linger in this part of Scotland. The River Clyde, originally scooped out from a shallow, fast-running salmon stream, is a dirty ditch of water lined with often weedy slips down which the proud new ships were once launched. Too many of the forested cranes are rusty and workless. Freighters still come into the docks around the Firth, but others rot mournfully in mid stream. The outstanding strength left in this place is the most awful of all. Up in one of the nearby lochs (which hereabouts are salty fiords, penetrating into the largely-useless land) is a base for Britain's small fleet of nuclear-powered and nuclear-armed submarines, the only real teeth left in her once-proud Navy. But the nuclear warheads upon the devastating missiles that these craft carry are supplied to Britain as an outlying satellite power by the United States of America.

Once upon a time Glasgow would have shivered at the very thought of such a shame. Now she scarcely notices it.

The city is ringed by associated towns which were made wealthy once by great industries, nearly all of which have ceased disastrously to be prosperous. They have been beaten in price and speed of delivery by foreign competitors. The only comparatively bright spots are new town developments like Kilbride, thanks partly to the investment of American money in Scottish branches. But these suffer already from the Gorbals disease. There are continual strikes, which eventually not even American finance may be able to endure.

Every city, no matter how grim, has at least one so-called beauty spot, and that of Glasgow is Loch Lomond. The largest of the Scottish lakes, it is not even a pond by American standards, only twenty-three miles long and five miles wide at its fattest point. It is overlooked by the sometimes snow-capped Ben Lomond, a typically Scottish mountain just 3,192 feet high. It contains some thirty small islands and still a surprising number of the kind of fish which make angling worthwhile. It has, for some one hundred and fifty years, been Glasgow's principal playground, a short distance by even bicycle for the workers; and it is our introduction to the second Scotland which is the Highlands.

In no country is there a greater dichotomy between lowlands and highlands than in Scotland. The people of the plains have been mainly newcomers from southern and eastern lands and the other Celtic place across the western water which is Ireland. They have been the steady, hard workers and the creators and earners of industrial wealth. They have done all this out of a comparatively narrow strip of territory across Scotland's flat waistline.

We have already discussed the shepherds and the rustlers of the southern, border hills. The Highlanders are quite a different breed, tending to be dark and slim and tempestuous, living the narrow lives of sheep-raising mountaineers but always in such a highly poetical way that the world's image of Scotland is really a reflection of them and not of the more pedestrian and hard-working others. The kilt, the bagpipes, the whisky, the claymore, the legends, they all came from the Highlands originally.

Around Loch Lomond the true hills begin, purple and misty, clouded even to this day with the mystery of romance. The best of the songs started hereabouts. In fine weather it has something of the atmosphere of Central Park, because the Glasgow people plus a few wondering visitors are so obviously enjoying themselves for once, but in bad weather, which means most of the time, it can still be quite awful in its sad and miniature grandeur.

4

STIRLING AND PERTH

TOURISTS are told that Stirling is the gateway to the Scottish Highlands, and this is true in both the historical and tourist senses. The Castle on the high hill of Stirling kept the marauding Highlanders at bay in historical times. Seven of the battlefields upon which the old Scotland bled to death are within sight of the Castle on the rock. And the bus services, like Greyhounds of the north, usefully penetrate from Stirling up the lengthy glens into the Grampian Mountains and the remote regions of grouse and heather where men can still be found who behave like their past.

But there are many such Highland gateways, and Stirling is no longer advisedly the best. Like so much in the modern world, it has been overtrodden and commercialized. Even its history in the Castle walls has lost glamor with usage. The facilities of the town are not what they were. Too many bus parties have passed through them.

Perth and its surrounding areas is a much better bet. There are still some excellent hotels in the rich little city—enriched by several interesting industries, foremost among which are the distilling of whisky, cattle auctions, dyeing and dry-cleaning, ropemaking and insurance. The River Tay that threads an errant way through the sandstone architecture is one of the most beautiful in Scotland. It is good for salmon and disasters alike.

Perth was, until 1437, the proud capital of Scotland, and retains an atmosphere of aristocratic self-confidence. The Black Watch, its famous military regiment, was successfully present at more battles all over the world than any other martial formation devised by man. Nearby is the village of Scone with its ruins of the abbey and palace in which the ancient Scottish kings were crowned on "the stone of destiny," a stone which was yanked away by the English to become one more trophy in Westminster Abbey, London.

59

So much money was brought to Perth in the past by her nobles and soldiers and so much is brought even today by her well-based industries—so much more modest and surely-based than those of Glasgow—that the little city remains comfortable in its appointments and determinedly *alive*. It has the atmosphere of a busy market town. Every second person in the streets has obviously come in from the country for the day, and most are naturally or self-consciously Scottish.

The plain, natural farmers wear plain clothes and have hard faces. If you come to them as a salesman they will listen with Buster Keaton expressionlessness for half-an-hour and then say either "Nae" or "Aye." Most often it will be "Nae."

The self-conscious countryfolk are those of the upper class. They will even wear the kilt sometimes, although never gaudily in the street. That is to say they will wear only a plain-colored kilt, the tartan or chequered and striped pattern in several contrasting colors being reserved for ceremonial evening or military wear. The man who wears a tartan kilt with civilian clothing in the daytime is as socially objectionable as the Englishman once was who wore brown shoes with a dark suit or the Texan who rides to the rodeo in a Derby hat.

This, like most strange customs, has a definite historical origin. The Scottish tartan goes back to the dim beginnings of the so-called "Celts" near what we now describe as Asia Minor. In the fifteenth century it became, as worn in the form of kilts and plaids, almost a uniform of the Highland clans or tribes. Each tribal chieftain had his own tartan designed and only his family and/or followers could wear it.

In those sword-clashing battles of the remote *Macbeth* period men would literally die for the sake of their tartan. (That was foolish enough but was it more foolish than dying just for the sake of passing another car on the Thruway?)

When the English finally crushed the Scots in 1745 they had to make sure that the fire would never ignite in the heather again. In those days the English were like the Russians in such countries as Czechoslovakia. So the English, together with many other coldly-calculated acts of deliberate repression, made it illegal for Scots to wear their tartans anymore.

The new aristocracy in Scotland then became the people who collaborated with the English and of course they obeyed their masters and wore only plain-colored kilts and plaids.

By 1782 a subject people was so convinced of the folly of further resistance—and becoming so tied up with the English in the commercial sense anyway—that it was quite safe for the English to be benevolent suddenly and remove many of the restrictions on the Scots, including the law about wearing the tartan.

But to this day well-bred Scots in the streets of Perth wear only plain-colored tweeds; and anyone in a tartan kilt is either a member of the Black Watch Regiment or a nice American tourist trying to do in Rome as Rome doesn't.

Harris tweeds in faded tints of green and brown provide the garb for the aristocratic countryfolk who come in to spend the day shopping and doing business in Perth. Also handmade brogue shoes of real leather and either tweed caps, flattened to the peaks, or pork-pie tweed Fedoras. The sole concession to the revolution in masculine appearances that has taken place elsewhere in the world will perhaps be rather self-conscious sideburns—but these of course probably originated in Perth in the first place, during the centuries when all Highlanders were hairy.

The women of these fine, tall men wear the same tweeds and stride even more manfully along the streets. The more dashing will sometimes sport a plain felt hat with a capercailzie feather stuck into the ribbon band. (The capercailzie is what the countryfolk still call the capercaillie or Scandinavian wood grouse, one of Scotland's game birds).

Inside their houses the women wear tweed skirts, well below the bony knee whatever is the fashion, and cashmere twin sets of either bottle green or oatmeal color.

But they are delightful women, among the world's nicest. They speak a very clear version of English with lilting accents. The musical voices rise at the end of each word like a Frenchman's. Nice homely Scottish dialect words like "bonny" and "braw" and "awfu'" and "lassie" give the talk a childishly romantic tinge. Then, whatever their wealth or social position or lack of it, they greet the stranger without either chill or surliness. They are friendly without being repulsive and the world must naturally love them. The man who goes to this little country and finds himself a Scottish wife stands a very good chance of being comfortable and happy for the rest of his life.

Or that was the position until recently. It may be changed overnight in an age of tumbling institutions everywhere. It may have changed already.

All the same it might be predicted that when the world is finally in ruins it will be a good Scots wife who will best be able to help a really determined man to survive it.

Perth owes her comparative perfection to the same refusal to grow too big that has made Switzerland such an excellent country. Even to this day Switzerland will rigorously pass laws to prevent population increases and to curtail economic expansion. In Perth throughout the ages when men have come out with too ambitious projects the wiseheads have shaken those heads and refused permission.

Consequently the three main hotels are of the nice kind that have never grown too big, and there are no skyscrapers or vast industrial areas. The city remains a small market town not only in size but also in spirit and it is possible to walk about freely there without fear of the kind of sudden death that stalks the streets of the greater metropolises of the world.

The shops are predominantly of the kind that are presided over by salty local characters and that feature the goods most wanted by hard-working and prosperous countryfolk. It is possible to buy the best in leather gloves and in tobaccos blended on the premises by a man whose great-great-grandparents first started the shop.

The best Harris tweed, as sold usefully in several shops of Perth and similar Scottish towns, is still woven on traditional looms by the crofters of the Outer Hebrides, islands off the north-west coast, from wool of the Blackfaced or Cheviot sheep. The genuine variety can be identified by the trademark affixed which shows the round orb surmounted by Celtic cross, and the quality remains constant in an increasingly meretricious world.

All this is better than the actual history in Perth, which, as in most places elsewhere, has become trodden down flat by too much guide-book writing and the over-neat habits of city councils combined with outright hard selling. The tourist who arrives in a package will, for example, be constrained to visit the famous "Fair Maid's House," supposedly where the heroine of Sir Walter Scott's *Fair Maid of Perth* actually lived. But of course the book was a work of fiction, and only those with the liveliest of imaginations can get any real satisfaction from surveying this grim little dwelling where the souvenir sellers still ply a lively trade.

Bridgend House in Main Street and No. 10, Rose Terrace, were childhood homes of that flatulent Victorian writer John Ruskin, but does that really mean anything to anybody today?

It might just be worth visiting St. John's Church with its fifteenth century tower, at St. John's Place in the centre of the city, because the tombstone of King James I's grave is there and John Knox once preached a violent sermon against idolatry above a congregation which soon made him an object of idolatry himself.

The local people in Perth get their outdoor pleasures from fishing in the River Tay and from playing games and strolling on the two Inches. These are flat pieces of public grassland, emerald green as only the lawns of Celtic lands can be. The "Celts" were often driven by tougher peoples into remote lands with bad climates, but had their compensations, notably those enjoyed in agriculture from continually warm rainfalls induced by the Gulf Stream Drift. The South Inch has only the usual Scott monument to make it famous, but the North Inch can sometimes inspire an imaginative and learned man to those traditional thoughts which "run too deep for tears." Here in the olden days raged one of the most notable clan battles in all Scottish history (described of course by Scott, once and for all in the *Fair Maid*). No fewer than thirty champions from the Clan Chattan and the Clan Quhele met each other in bloody mortal combat, and there are still foolish poets who say that the grass grew significantly greener afterwards.

But today the names Chattan and Quhele are both forgotten, maybe because like prehistoric monsters the breeding bulls of those tribes killed each other off—and if there is any real fighting hereabouts it is on the adjacent golf course, which in its way is more historic and important than that of St. Andrew's. Modern golf more or less started there, when the invention of gunpowder put the local bow-and-arrow makers out of work and they turned to the making of golf clubs instead. (Before gunpowder the Scottish rulers had actually tried to make the game illegal, because they thought that the English beat their archers who had been practising golf instead of archery).

One of the most common and famous names in these parts is Dewar, which in its correct form should be Deuchar. There were two really important Dewars. One of them, from Kincardine to the south, invented not only the thermos flask but also the explosive known as cordite. The other did not invent whisky, but, with the aid of the excellent Perth water and the rich barley as grown in the nearby river valley known as the Garse of Gowrie, made such a delectable commercial variety of the brew in the nineteenth century that one of Britain's most important export industries was thereby given much impetus. His descendants became ennobled and his enterprise joined others to form the immense Distillers Company, comprising such as "Haig" (most popular in Britain itself), "Vat 69" and "Black and White" (especially liked in Germany), "Johnnie Walker" and "Dewars" (favorites in North America), and "White Horse" (which naturally does best in South Africa). "Johnnie Walker" is the world best-seller.

The writer has savored just two supremely potent brands of whisky in his time. One was a specially-reserved bottle of Dewar's "Ancestor," opened by that notable breeder of Aberdeen-Angus cattle Willie Reid, at Fordhouse of Dun near Montrose. Another was a misty Glenlivet far to the north, and that shall be described later. Both were twice as strong as the pale stuff offered minutely in London, and their effect was to induce an euphoria beside which the accounts of those who prefer LSD sound like the day dreams of half-starved spinsters.

So Perth, if it has produced only this finely-distilled spirit, is always to be remembered along with the Côte d'Or and Parnassus.

It has produced much more than that. The local beer alone is almost unequalled in most men's experience. It is served in large glasses like German beer and the head is carefully pared away by wooden spatulas until only a quarter of an inch of pure cream remains. The substance of the brew is rich; and a dram of whisky chased by a pint of it is at once more stimulating and at the same time more sedative than all the doctor's carefully-prescribed pep pills and tranquillizing drugs.

Whisky is spelt "whiskey" with an "e" only in lesser places without the law where they also try to make it, such as Ireland and the two countries of the North American continent. And the name is a corruption of "usquebaugh," itself derived from the original Gaelic words "wisge-beatha," which may be nicely translated as "water of life."

It is highly significant also that Perth is the home of one of Britain's soundest insurance corporations. The contribution of the Scots to modern methods of finance is the greatest of any people save the Lombards and the Jews. It is not too much to say that our banking and insurance systems, our investment trusts and methods of credit expansion (the creation of money out of nothing) would never have come into existence but for the parsimonious ingenuity of what the eighteenth and nineteenth centuries called North Britons. The great Bank of England itself, as well as the idea of a permanent National Debt—they were, of course, the brain children of a typical small town Scot, William Paterson.

Money in our present location of Perth does not, however, obtrude. The millionaire storekeeper who lives in one of the big houses on the hill overlooking the little city most discreetly keeps his half-dozen or so large automobiles locked away in a barnlike garage among the garden tools. The sole real evidence of wealth locally is cattle.

From the earliest periods of human history true wealth has been partly measured in terms of livestock, and, until we devise satisfactory synthetic foods, it will continue to be so. Here in Perth is the world marketing center of two of the most important cattle and several of the leading sheep breeds.

Every spring and fall the buyers come from the Americas as well as the farmlands of the Pacific (and increasingly from the Communist countries) to buy at the Perth sales of Macdonald, Fraser and Company young bulls and heifers of the Aberdeen-Angus and Scotch Shorthorn breeds. They pay for young beasts, often under a year old, what would be a fortune to most people. They take these away to their distant prairies like a motorist periodically tops up his battery with new distilled water. Because they have found not only that the best beef cattle blood comes from Scotland but also that it needs constant reinforcement.

There is something in the very soil of the Scottish pastoral areas that produces cattle whose flesh and bone has incomparable quality. Once away from Scotland those beasts tend to decline, and after a few generations they can even become dwarfish and sterile. (Does the same apply to men from the North?) So, to maintain their herds in good condition the Argentinians and the Texans and the Australians must come to Perth and spend kings' ransoms on beautiful little animals.

Yes, they are no longer rangy great bulls and cows. The extremely clever Scottish specialists in animal breeding have brought down the animals to their commercial essentials, producing them just for good, lean beef and the ability to transmit this characteristic to offspring.

The outstandingly important breed at Perth is the Aberdeen-Angus, called thus because it flourishes best in the neighboring counties of Aberdeenshire and Angus. It is a queer beast, polled or hornless since faded, ancient days when no records were kept save on sculptured stones. It is jet black and strangely primeval in appearance, rather like a folk memory carved in basalt. A joint of meat from these animals should be nicely cherry-colored and laced with useful thin marblings of white fat, which melt in the oven and help to cook the flesh without basting.

The cattle breeders of this part of Scotland work on records that go back a long time. Generally speaking the craft is a modern one statistically, but the pedigrees of some Aberdeen-Angus families go back well over two hundred years. The male is all-important for transmitting characters, and must be homozygous (or predominant over the female in passing down his traits), but, curiously enough, the true pedigrees trace back what are known as the "families" of the females, Ericas, Cherry Blossoms and the like, all stemming from one original and especially excellent cow.

Some time is being devoted to this rather offbeat subject because it may one day be of vital importance indeed. American research has recently demonstrated that modern man, breeding promiscuously, is deteriorating so rapidly thanks to the encouragement of recessive genes that before very long he will be unable to control his environment successfully anymore. Unless he does something about it he will become extinct. And what he eventually does will be what the Scots have so finely done with animals. The research teams who work on the salvation of mankind will just have to come to Perth.

The Scotch Shorthorn is more "familiar" in appearance than the Aberdeen-Angus. It has the dun-red and white coloring, the sharp, short horns and curly hair of the bulls in comic strips and the cows who used to dominate the small dirt farms of the old western world. In our recent, specialized age it has tended to lack supporters compared with the Aberdeen-Angus for quality beef on one side and the Hereford for quick-growing rough beef on the other. But at the Perth sales it is still a very important animal, and there are certain Scottish breeders who are currently developing a hornless variety that should soon be predominant.

The best of Perthshire is a lovely, fertile valley between low, blue mountains. Maybe this plain is one of the best strips of pastoral land in the world, being based as most of the best are on red sandstone. In places the climate is good enough to enable soft fruits to be grown in commercial abundance; and they have a flavor that only the magic chemistry of the Scottish soil and weather can impart.

Between Perth and Stirling the westward part of this valley contains many, many farms which still produce the wonderful cattle; and the interesting feature of the region is that many are worked not by local peasants but by what the British call gentry. These are predominantly representatives of the former ruling class who, like Pre-Raphaelities, have found it best to go back to their origins and try again.

They are people like the former British Army officer and member of a Lloyd's insurance syndicate in London who bought a Perthshire farm and went to the sales and selected his basic Aberdeen-Anguses so cleverly that they eventually swelled into one of the most successful herds of the breed. The several sons of his best bull were sold in one year for the kind of money that only Americans can understand.

Or the aristocratic ladies who established a herd nearby and similarly won most of the prizes. Extreme cleanliness was the feature of their farm, which stood out even in a land where the farmers have always needed to be thorough in order to survive. In a small ship or a small country it is not a virtue to be tidy and clean: it is a grim necessity.

Perhaps the most important Aberdeen-Angus breeder of all time was a man who lived in a castle and was deliberately rude to strangers and over-careful with his money. These qualities enabled him to breed animals perfectly, from cattle to horses, and including farm-yard poultry. He gave no pleasure to his immediate contacts but to the wider world he gave Aberdeen-Anguses without compare, includ-ing a distinct line of all-important females.

Another very successful herd in this region was created by a man and wife who also ran cinemas in Glasgow; and there was a baronet who drove his own tractors and worked harder than anybody else on his farm. His Scotch Shorthorns achieved the same high fame as those of a young man whose ancestors had built an enormous steel empire, or another who got his from butchers' shops. A financier with a household name devoted much of his old age to swaggering around a Perthshire model farm with a crooked stick in his hand, and to choosing the best newborn calves for breeding.

All were, and are, hospitable as only Americans can be elsewhere. They possess no English reticences, and they extend friendly hands to every comer. While other people are seeking just an end to work and more money (thus devaluing their true incomes) these fine relics of the past labor long hours and their only holidays are at the cattle sales and shows. Their chief interest in life is the betterment of a breed of animals (and maybe they instinctively feel that when the world falls around them it is possible that they can survive).

A feature of this phenomenon in modern Scotland is that it might never have arisen but for the English tax laws, cunningly designed to favor those who put back money into the land. But for those laws the cattle breeders might have been just those real local farmers whose herds can be as important as those of the gentry. It is doubtful, how-ever, if the farmers would have got half so far but for the stimulus of the tax-avoiding money. Bureaucrats who devise governmental impositions sometimes do not know exactly how much real good they are doing.

5

FIFE AND ANGUS

BELOW Perth and towards the east are two quite different areas, the county of Kinross and the ancient Kingdom of Fife. And, north and east of Perth, is Angus.

There is little of interest in Kinross save its size and a nice, Highland-type road through a glen of trees and rushing river, where Perthshire comes south to the Ochil Hills.

The size of Kinross makes it notable because it is the smallest county of Scotland, only 82 square miles. Its population is under 7000 and its largest conurbation has only some 2,400 fortunate souls. Are they happier than the millions of Tokyo? Maybe not; but at least they are never likely to be obliterated by the inexorable law of Malthus. (Population increases mean periodic population checks, if not by moral restraint then by inevitable disaster: Thomas Robert Malthus, British economist, 1766–1834.)

The history hounds will, however, turn the car eastwards in the village of Kinross and follow the bloody trail to equally little Loch Leven, upon the shores of which they will brood suitably over the melancholy fate of one of their old favorites, Mary Queen of Scots.

Loch Leven is only six square miles in area but contains a considerable quantity of excellent trout as well as many miniscule islands, on one of which, Castle Island, will be seen the drear ruins of the fortress in which Mary was imprisoned. Her true story will be outlined later, but imaginative visitors to this place will recall the evening of May 2, 1568, when the romantic, sexy young Queen, after eleven months of imprisonment under dour Douglases here, characteristically won the heart of Willie Douglas, a boy of 16, so that he procured her escape in a small boat after setting the other boats adrift and locking the castle gates and throwing away the keys.

That is all Kinross, and maybe it has been enough to procure it the kind of immortality that makes Shakespeares write and Hollywoods film.

The ancient Kingdom of Fife really has much more to offer. It is a fat peninsula jutting into the North Sea or former German Ocean with the Firth of Tay to the north and the Firth of Forth to the south. (A firth is what they call in Scotland an arm of the sea or an estuary; and the word derives from the original Scottish mispronunciation of the Scandinavian "fiord.")

Fife starts with the Forth Bridge from near Edinburgh, the iron and cantilever railway bridge, not the road crossing opened in 1964. This iron masterpiece, finished 1890, is one of the few monuments of industriousness and engineering that survive from the Victorian age (a survival, however, that depends upon constant and costly repainting). Like the Eiffel Tower of Paris it represents a gigantic nineteenth century object not only of technological mastery but also of sheer beauty. The engineers responsible for its construction knew exactly what they were doing and did it perfectly. The beauty is that of function.

To be a boy once and to get up early on the Aberdeen train from London and peer out of the window at the finny ripples of the Firth of Forth what seemed a mile below, and then up at the girders which entangled the sky, was to be present at the dawn of a new world. Also it inculcated a pride that would survive a whole lifetime of disasters. No doubt they would construct a larger Golden Gate Bridge in the far West, and Sydney in Australia would divise its gigantic coathanger, but no one would ever beat the Scots when it came to a matter of sheer engineering.

No matter that the actual engineers in this case were Englishmen. They were Sir John Fowler and Sir Benjamin Baker, also responsible for London's first Tube or deep underground railway. (It was Baker who designed the Aswan Dam in Egypt). The actual job was done in Scotland, mainly by Scotsmen. They cast a network of steel girders over 150 feet high above the mile-wide channel of the Forth, in 26 spans of which the main ones were each 1,710 feet in length. They used 54,000 tons of steel and 6½ million rivets and—final triumph in this part of the world—the entire work cost only some 12 million dollars (and is as strong and practicable and beautiful today as it was when opened over 80 years ago).

Alas, they did not build a *road* bridge over the wide Forth until it was almost too late and Britain had nearly foundered anyway. In the nineteenth century they knew that bridges must be built to accommodate the railroad. In the twentieth century they allowed the motor roads to meander still; and grotesque car ferries created frustrating

A contrast in bridgework. The new road and the old railway links across the Forth.

delays over this vital Forth link during 50 years of increasingly intensive traffic.

That fatal defect of spirit can be observed even more gloomily once the Forth is crossed. Now the wonderful anchorage of Rosyth contains only the grey ghosts of the thousands of warships which once harbored here. This was in its time a great naval base which cost myriads of dollars to build and maintain. Its conditions of depth, tide and security were perfect. After the Second World War there was just an increasing run-down, till eventually only rats scuttled amid many of the immense docks, submarine basins, oil tanks, workshops, sheds of millionaire stores. Britain no longer ruled the waves.

Dunfermline, inland from Rosyth, is sadly again the sort of place where giant phantoms tread the stony ways of ultimate decadence. This was a proud capital city as long ago as the eleventh century. The Abbey was founded by Malcolm Canmore, who became King of Scotland in 1054. He married that remarkable Margaret, granddaughter of Edmund Ironside, who was canonized as a saint by the Roman Catholic Church not only because she gave it a lot of money but also because she worked so hard to civilize the crude aborigines of the

Scottish Lowlands. She and her husband are bones in St. Margaret's Shrine here.

Dunfermline Abbey was the burial place of Robert the Bruce, remote progenitor not only of the British Royal Family but also of the present Earls of Elgin and Kincardine. Robert the Bruce illustrated a facet of the Scottish character when he watched a spider try, try, try again and decided to do the same himself. He was one of the few Scotsmen ever to defeat the English, and eventually he made himself King of a temporarily united land. His descendants played an enormous part in the eventual creation of the British Empire. Queen Elizabeth the Second and Prince Philip the Duke of Edinburgh both have his blood, and those other Bruces, the Earls of Elgin, not only embellished the British Museum with splendid ancient marbles found in an untidy heap at the Parthenon in Athens and bought for about 140,000 dollars, but eventually played a large part in the creation of major Scottish industries. That pleasant and industrious man, the present Earl, has run a pedigree herd, a tourist hotel and other desperate enterprises to survive.

Dunfermline Abbey suffers from an indigestion of royal tombs, not only Robert's but also those of Donald III, Edgar, Alexander I and III,

One of the wonders of the 19th. century world and of every Scottish childhood: the Forth Bridge which carries the railroad from Edinburgh to Fife.

David I and Malcolm IV. Malcolm's Tower in Pittencrieff Park and Wallace Well are relics of a once-royal palace wherein three notable kings were born.

The Public Library in Dunfermline contains one of the finest collections of Robert Burns' works; and rightly so since it was munificently given to the town, also Pittencrieff Park itself and much else, by that Andrew Carnegie who was in his way the Robert Bruce of a different age.

No. 4, Moodie Street, Dunfermline, is one more of those low stone hovels which, in Scotland, mean more than vast cathedrals or heady skyscrapers. For there was a brief period in the history of this curious country, a period of flowering, when to get suitably born in such a poverty-stricken cottage meant ultimate achievement indeed. Either you became a world-famous writer or, eventually, towards the end of the period, a multi-millionaire.

It could be demonstrated that among the gravest errors of our age has been the deliberate improvements in the conditions of the poor which has made it impossible anymore for such people as Burns and Carlyle and Carnegie and Charlie Chaplin to achieve their fame and

The new Forth road bridge, built after generations of procrastination, has the longest suspension span in Europe.

make their millions. Cunningly-devised taxation has been partly responsible for this, also a cleverly-inculcated shame in the very idea of the impoverished beginning. The enormous policy-making of the Soviet Union has perhaps most of all destroyed the soil in which such great and fruitful men can flower.

If modern Russia had possessed just one Andrew Carnegie it would be a much happier and more prosperous country today. It would certainly have experienced no lack of either consumer goods on the one side or honest books and fearless readers on the other.

Carnegie came out of that Dunfermline hovel a hard, determined youngster who rapidly rose from telegraph boy to superintendent of a railroad when taken by his parents to Pittsburgh. He introduced the first sleeping-cars, then made a small fortune out of oil, and, still a very young man, smashed all his competitors to form a vast empire out of the local iron and steel industries. His flint eyes and zipped mouth did not just defeat all softer operators and trades unionists. They forced the growth of modern America's industrial might.

The man was an ogre, a capitalist, a self-crowned king before whom all humanity was subservient. He eventually became worth much more money than all the Caesars and Napoleons of history. And what did he do with it?

His benefactions ranged from a 3 million dollar trust fund for his native city of Dunfermline to free public libraries for most of the English-speaking countries. The fund, he said, might bring "more sweetness and light" into the "monotonous lives of the toiling masses." The libraries certainly enabled a lot of earnest people to acquire too much of the little knowledge which is a dangerous thing, but, how useful they were to us as boys!

Emerging from his Dunfermline hovel Carnegie gave the world modern steel and the basis of the the American ability to save the world from alien tyrannies. Also he gave it, for better or for worse, the public library system and many, many other benefactions, ranging from the endowment of universities to the construction of Carnegie Hall in New York. He was a pioneer in trying to make people get up early for work and stop smoking, and he devoted himself exclusively in his old age to trying to convince his fellow men that they should abandon the madness of war and work for an international political system that would guarantee peace.

Today such self-willed men are as unlikely to re-emerge as the dinosaur again, and so are their industrial achievements and social benefactions.

Go to Dunfermline today and it will be found that Carnegie's cottage at No. 4, Moodie Street, is crammed from top to bottom with illuminated addresses and caskets and cups and medals from all parts of the world, given to the poor boy eventually as a small expression of humanity's gratitude.

The reason he gave Pittencrieff to the town as a public park, he once said, was that as a small boy he could only look at it through railings and now he wanted all the people to enjoy what was denied to him. It does seem indeed that the true socialist turns out to be the masterful, overriding capitalist.

The guide books drool in Fife over the historic memories of Dunfermline, and the university and golf courses of St. Andrews, and they point out that the county town (which means the administrative center) is Cupar. This Cupar is variously described as pleasantly small and yet "up-to-date," with such industries as linen, sugar beet, tanning and coach building. It is in reality quite deadly in greystone appearance, and overcrowded with ill-regulated miniature car traffic.

St. Andrews, on the contrary, most definitely has something, although exactly what that is will always be difficult to state. For the sensitive it is neither the "ancient" university nor the golfing associations.

Scots often point proudly to St. Andrews as their oldest university, but the facts should be clearly understood that although a bishop started a college there in 1410, just before other churchmen, not to be outdone, established the foundations of colleges at Glasgow and Aberdeen, yet the institution never flourished, and completely died when its Catholic organizers were expelled at the Reformation. It was not revived until the late nineteenth century and then principally as a sort of glorified girls' school. It slowly became the nucleus at least of a proper university but was split in two parts after the last war, by far the most vigorous because scientific part being located in Dundee, across the water north.

The feminine element is still very strong in St. Andrews. About half the students are mini-skirted (beneath rather charming black gowns with scarlet lined hoods). But the university as such is neither wholly viable in the academic sense nor worthy to be regarded as a historic seat of ancient tradition. Many American universities have longer continuity as well as real size (St. Andrews accommodates only about 2,600 young people).

No doubt there are those to whom the Royal and Ancient Golf Club of St. Andrews is a shrine equivalent to what Jerusalem was to Crusaders in the Middle Ages or the ruins of Hollywood to very young film critics today. Those would be people to whom golf is something more than the world's most exasperating waste of precious time ever invented. There are balls, there are sticks to hit them, and there are red-faced, cursing men: also astronomical bills at the nineteenth hole.

And maybe St. Andrews' claim to have invented it all, in spite of the fact that the game came first from Holland probably and took real Scottish root at Perth, would be more cogent if only the people of the town and other Scotsmen could play it more successfully. Americans come over to the grand tournaments, Americans representing all the races of the world intermingled, and they consistently break the records and win the prizes.

It is, like so much else in an old country, largely a matter of making money out of dubious history, but what money! St. Andrews, a town of no more than 10,000 inhabitants, has as many as four 18-hole golf courses (the Old, the New, the Eden and the Jubilee) and it is plastered with putting greens, studded with club houses, and completely entangled in the rules and regulations that, by tradition, are made here for the golf world and here alone. The rather nice old hotels cluster around the sacred lawns and warlike bunkers like hags around a corpse.

A very pleasant holiday could be spent in one of these hotels, probably as pleasant as anywhere in Scotland save perhaps Kelso or Turnberry or Birnam whose woods came down to Dunsinane. The visitor, provided he did not play golf or seek the higher learning, could live in a vacuum of complete strangeness. Some nice Scots and Americans would talk to him, but he would be left out of the essential life of the place, and would thus be able to observe all the better what actually makes it tick.

It is not the ancient college buildings and ruins of the abbey, and Queen Mary's House, and what remains of the finest cathedral in Scotland. It is not the Martyr's Monument, where once they burned the religious maniacs, nor yet Witch Hill where they formerly fried the nastier of the local women.

It is not even the memorial fountain in Market Street to that Major Whyte-Melville who actually achieved fame with a book called *Black, but Comely*.

It is the situation of St. Andrews, the sandscape by the sea, and the brisk, maritime air.

This air and delectable salt scenery really begins with Fife. They can be experienced on the coast south of the Firth of Forth which extends to North Berwick and then drops to such preliminary fishing ports as Dunbar. But the true magic of north-eastern, Scandinavian Scotland begins with the yellow shores of strange Fife, where seaside names like Dysart, Leven, Elie, Pittenweem, Anstruther and Crail most perfectly express what can still be felt there: the keen, keen air, the sands strewn like a fair boy's hair, sands up which the viking boats ploughed to disgorge their hordes of red-barbed predators.

This atmosphere is finally civilized and preserved in the golden amber of the occasional sun at St. Andrews, some of which faces almost due north towards the Arctic Ocean. It is a stimulating and wonderful and often beautiful atmosphere, which, like a little Bovril of our childhood, can quickly put a man on his feet. (Bovril was and is a meat essence in a small brown bottle, but once achieved fame in Britain with one of the first of the really great advertising campaigns, that showed a young bull snorting and chasing a red-faced, sturdy invalid).

Not many places ever achieve real atmosphere, but St. Andrews is among them.

Quite unlike Kirkcaldy, the real capital and only important town of Fife, and that in spite of the fact that Kirkcaldy has an actual physical atmosphere from the smell of the linoleum and oil-cloth which are traditionally manufactured here. Kirkcaldy is rich and hardworking and vigorously alive where the other towns of Fife are deadly or artificial, but no one could accuse it of possessing the strange, almost spiritual beauty of a St. Andrews. It is industrial and unashamed of it, and leads to the Fife coal mines which once supplied Scotland with a considerable part of its wealth but are no longer wanted anymore by shortsighted governments.

Kirkcaldy, like the Forth Bridge, represents still the nineteenth century industrial energy of Britain, and was suitably the birthplace of that Adam Smith the pioneer economist, whose *Wealth of Nations* led to the way we are running the world wrongly now. It was natural that the earnest Thomas Carlyle should go there to live for a while and that the United Free Church should have Burne-Jones windows.

Even the great Robert, of the Adam architectural brothers, was born but most certainly did not stay there.

Far better to continue up the coast to that little Crail which has been mentioned before. It is nearly to Fife Ness, and this projects from the pennisula finally into the herring-grey sea. There are a small harbor, sandy bays with picturesque rocks of the kind that overhang marvellous anemone pools, and fishermen's cottages with red roofs still. All the buildings are similarly old and curious, especially the Town House with its Dutch tower. A Blue Boulder by the churchyard gate was traditionally flung by the Devil from the nearby Isle of May in an abortive effort to frustrate the building of Crail Kirk.

Also for the practised connoisseur in resortmanship there are the inevitable and ineffable golf, putting and bathing (the last, of course, for real lunatics in this clime).

Leuchars, up beyond St. Andrews, was notable for one of the cleanest and tastiest fish-and-chip shops of all Britain, run by an Italian family (maybe it still is) and for the aerodrome from which a few youngsters once mounted in primitive machines to save their country from German invasion.

So we come to the "mighty Tay Bridge."

Once again the adjective is used for the railway bridge, although the car crosses a new road bridge opened in 1966 after several generations of argument as to whether it was really necessary.

This enormous railway bridge of 86 spans, that crosses two miles of what amounts to turbulent sea near the mouth of the Firth of Tay, is notable as one more great nineteenth century achievement. It possesses neither the beauty nor the sheer engineering charm of the Forth Bridge. But it is famous because children in the wormlike trains upon it once, and indeed today, could and can stare down in suitable awe upon the remains in the rough water at the side of the *first* Tay Bridge, which, soon after Christmas on December 28, 1879, in the midst of a great gale in unholy torrential rain and darkness, was partly swept away. As a result the thundering northbound train that night plunged complete into the gap and down, down into the lashing waves where it was swallowed up and disappeared completely save for a last gasp of steam and some wreckage that usefully strewed the Angus beaches next day. There were some 90 passengers in that train and naturally most of them were never seen again, but the popular prints made so much of it, thanks to graphic artist and the journalistic flair of Dundee in particular, that no one in Britain could grow up between 1879 and 1939 without regarding this event as one of the most awfully spectacular in modern history. (After 1939 the whole course of history irremediably changed.)

Nevertheless the protruding piers of the old bridge can still be seen, and it is still possible to write about the event which they commemorate.

So we come to Angus, which in many ways is one of the most unspoilt and interesting counties of central Scotland, provided too much time is not spent in its single metropolis, bonny Dundee.

The little city is still bonny all right. It is not repellent as an industrial town, distinguished in the last century for its jam, jute and journalists; and the docks and fishermen's smells creep right into the heart of it, so that salt flavors the hungry lips everywhere. Good hotels include one run by a family with the most delightfully old-fashioned of furnishings and porters and typical Scots high teas with "haddie" (smoked haddock) and many kinds of flour buns with intriguing names such as "baps," "bannocks," and even "softies." It was possible to come down to breakfast and to be greeted by a rosy-cheeked serving lassie with the strange query "D'ye weesh fleaks?" (Readers can be left to work that one out for themselves, as the author was).

The jam manufacturing of Dundee began with the soft fruits that grow so finely and abundantly in this otherwise keen part of Scotland. The various jute-based industries probably began when local ships had to bring something back in their holds after mercantile ventures to far-distant India. And there is no particular reason why journalists from this city should always have been so lively unless it is in the tradition of the famous local *People's Journal*. In that case the great original man was one D. C. Thomson, who founded this paper in 1858 together with several other publications and finally a string of children's comics which probably had more influence on the education of the British young in the first half of the twentieth century than all the acts of Parliament and earnest schoolmasters.

Dundee is indeed so large and successful and lively that to stay long in it is unfair to the real rural Angus outside. It is like being detained in London before a true knowledge of Britain can be obtained. The municipal architecture so perfectly tells the story of Scotland's successes and excesses since 1800. There is the Royal Arch, an ornate structure in Dock Street which commemorates Queen Victoria's first visit to Dundee in 1844. The Caird Hall in City Square is a perfect example of the pseudo-classic style which ennobles city halls and their occupants everywhere. Castle Street has the premises where James Chalmers invented the adhesive postage stamp, and of course another building contains stained glass not only by Burne-Jones but also by William Morris this time. (How those Englishmen did range in their canny business!)

The modernized home of Graham of Claverhouse will be found in Dudhope Park. He was the gallant rebel against William and Mary in the seventeenth century who was killed at the unfortunate battle of Killiecrankie by, it has always been alleged, the only possible missile which could defeat him, a silver bullet.

One can brood in Dudhope Park not only over the melancholy fate of Claverhouse but also over an aviary, an aquarium and a monkey-house.

Angus, with its lovely Sidlaw Hills, lies nicely between the boisterous sea and the true Scottish Highlands. It is nearly always possible to stare upwards and north-west at the purple-blue of low, mysterious, and heather-covered mountains. The world is temporarily left behind if the road be taken from Dundee to Glamis. Only farms line the smooth macadam, with magnificent cattle and sheep, and, in season, such raspberries as grow in their sweetness nowhere else at all. And at Glamis there are two wonders, which will suitably impress the mind of the beholder according to his sense of values.

Glamis Castle is traditionally the scene of King Duncan's murder in his sleep by one of his generals, the wife-enraged Macbeth. And it actually looks like it still, a fairy castle of dreams and nightmares combined, all turreted and pointed and crenellated, wherefrom the Earls of Strathmore have ruled the neighbor lands for so many years that only legend can tell the beginning. Such events have occurred here as sometimes make the very stones look blood-red in the stern northern sunsets. There is, for example, the dread secret of Glamis

A typical Aberdeen-Angus champion as bred by R. B. Crockatt, The Peebles, Angus. Note the fine head, straight back, and blocky hindquarters. This is one of the things that Scotland can do better than any other country in the world.

that only the heir apparent can be told, and that on his twenty-first birthday.

The architecture of Glamis, like that of most inhabited castles and large country houses in Scotland, is strangely soft for such legends. Surely they did not build like that in the really bad old days? They did not. Glamis, like so many others, was completely remodelled in the seventeenth century in the style of a French chateau. But for the mist and the mystery it might have sprouted up suddenly like a mushroom in the Loire valley.

There are still at the time of writing some vigorous members of the Strathmore family in Glamis, and Britain's ruling Queen is partly a child of that family. Her mother was a Strathmore and born there. The Princess Margaret also first saw the light of day in that pile. And the rare art treasures and other antiques within would make a nice average week's shipment from Europe for any New York wholesale dealer.

Glamis is thus a heart of the matter in the real Scotland, especially if the visitor be privileged to regard at the same time the famous farm and cattle herds of Newhouse of Glamis nearby, which the writer of this book once knew intimately as representative of the very best in his country. That great man, physically as well as professionally, whom all could call Bob Adam, not only bred here the most important Aberdeen-Angus bulls of his time, as well as other animal breeds, but also maintained such a model of a farm that there was no dirt or disarray in it anywhere.

And when that is said does it make the reader suitably flinch at once? No dirt or disarray—how repellent and ugly and indeed anti-social! We all know today that the best food comes from a dirty kitchen and that when the Swiss trains run on time they are somehow horrible.

Maybe our age is right in its reassessment of what is good and proper in society, but the fact remains that perfectly-run Newhouse of Glamis is a record prize-winner in the breeding of supreme cattle at least; and the reader might be asked gently if he would not choose such a man as the famous Bob Adam to steer him to the stars or to perform a vital operation on his guts rather than an unpunctual, unmeticulous, filthy and anarchic exponent of complete social despair.

Indeed it is good country, this Angus, for getting down to fundamentals. From Glamis the sweet-scented road should be followed the few miles to Kirriemuir and at all costs a night should be spent there in the well-named Airlie Arms. This inn was nicely "unimproved" when last visited and had all the atmosphere of an ancient Scottish

Glamis Castle, Angus, a perfect example of the Scottish Baronial style, dating from the days when they knew both how to build and how to be beautiful.

hostelry. The high tea was superb, and, down in the bar afterwards, over strong beer and malt whisky, a nice assortment of local men were all vigorously playing parts from Barrie.

Once again the really knowledgeable reader must probably wince. He will still know about James Barrie, the Scottish writer, but will have been educated to disapprove of him heartily, the once-famous sentimentalist who actually wrote that dangerous play for children called *Peter Pan,* dangerous not just for its soft lushness of sentiment but also for its extraordinary *sexual* undertones. It is about the boy who didn't want to grow up, and his mother-fixation, and all that sort of turgid Freudianism.

But it must be insisted here that Scotland cannot be understood without Barrie and that he is still preeminently *important.*

The author of *Peter Pan, The Little Minister, A Window in Thrums, The Admirable Crichton, Quality Street, Dear Brutus* and many other of the most successful plays and books of the first quarter of our twentieth century, was born at this Kirriemuir on May 9, 1860. His birthplace at 11 Brechin Road—bought and presented to the nation by a grateful compatriot—was and is another of those white-washed cottages containing rooms so low-ceilinged that a tall man must stoop to be comfortable in them.

Barrie's father was a poor handloom weaver, who contrived eventually to obtain a good clerical position for himself in a local linen factory, and at the same time to provide his seven surviving children with a good education and start in life. Kirriemuir is traditionally a town of hand-weavers, an offshoot of the nearby Forfar where cloth has been made since the dawn of British history.

Margaret Ogilvy, Barrie's mother, was the daughter of a stonemason, but had the Ogilvy name, and was a woman of rare refinement, typically influential upon a talented, over-sensitive son. (After her death he wrote a book about her. He was a born journalist. And it is one of the finest tributes ever paid to a parent by a child. If a modern American mother had such a book written about her today the author would probably be certified as really insane.)

It has been said that Margaret was an Ogilvy. That is the family name of the local Earls of Airlie, who have long controlled this district of Scotland and fructified it with their blood. It is a lovely name, and a sensible man could wish for no other. A famous modern scion of the family is not only married to a Princess of the British Royal Family but is one of the canniest business men in the city of London.

Wee Jamie Barrie, as he was called on account of his real shortness, went to a village school for the kind of educational groundwork that only Scotland could give in those days, and afterwards to academies at Glasgow, Forfar and Dumfries. His fellow pupils more often than not went bare-footed, the lucky little devils (no expensive visits to pedicures for them thereafter); school equipment was crude and even books were usefully scarce; but Scots boys and girls of that time rarely left school without knowing as much as it was good for them to know. Barrie was only one brilliant product of that system, which turned out so many successful and famous people.

Nevertheless wee Jamie as a short, dark and impish lad impressed neither his school fellows nor his parents as a great man to be. He loved pranks and fishing, and his young horror of the future was always that he might have to give up these pastimes and really go to work.

Those who until recently remembered him in Kirriemuir would say that wee Jamie was not only one of the principal organisers of the famous game of Smuggle the Geeg, or Smuggleerie, that consisted of forming sides and then chasing each other helter-skelter through every wynd and close of the town; but also he was one of the principal Kirriemuir exponents of Chickie Maillie. This was quite a good game. You obtained a reel of thread and a pin and a button, and crept some dark night to a cottage window. You so fixed the contrivance that by standing a distance from the window you could make the button tap monotonously against it.

A contemporary of Barrie's once said that the inhabitants of Forfar would be terrified by the frequent apparition of a spring-heeled Jack, who, clad in white, sprang out from dark places upon simple people:

> One night when the carrier's cart was on its way to Forfar passing by Zoar the ghostly figure sprang towards it from a shady corner of the roadside. It chanced that a lame worthy was seated by the driver, his crutch in hand, and as the apparition came towards them he swung his crutch at it to such purpose that he felled its substantial framework to the ground. Within the sheet behold two young "sackets," James Barrie and Adam Harrison!

Barrie, who could rarely be serious, deliberately encouraged the legend of his boyish waywardness; but there are other tales of his childhood which throw a clearer light on his later development. Back of his birthplace on Brechin Road may still be seen a little wash-house. In this, according to good authority, wee Jamie persuaded other children to dress up and join him in amateur theatricals. Then, when the play was over, he would run into the cottage and sit at his mother's knee while she told him tale after tale about life in Kirriemuir when she was a girl (and especially about the "Auld Lichts," who belonged to one of the staunchest and most peculiar of the many Scottish religious sects). Thus Barrie absorbed the lore that he later retold in his best prose works.

"I remember well his splendid essays in English, his compositions, his fluent pen, his command of language," said a man who went to the same school as Barrie in Dumfries. "He was gifted with an extraordinary power of expressing his thoughts on paper. But if my memory serves me well young Barrie worked only when he felt inclined."

This may be well believed, because although Barrie was never at the bottom of his school class, and obtained a middling degree at Edinburgh University, he did not win high academic honors. In fact his real literary career began when he wrote a letter to the editor of the Dumfries newspaper on the desirability of longer vacations from school. The publication of that letter made him realize that he could perhaps earn a living as a journalist. At the age of 23 he went down to that Nottingham in England which started by establishing the fame of Robin Hood and ended with such legendary literary figures as D. H. Lawrence, Cecil Roberts and Alan Sillitoe. The tradition of newspaper work there must have been akin to that of Boston and Dundee (and indeed, for that matter, remote Christchurch, New Zealand). So many of the men who passed through those hard schools could not fail to write eventually what the public wanted. They were trained that way.

After two years in Nottingham the little Scotsman had to come to London. Scotsmen at that time had to come to London as Americans later had to go to Paris (if only to sit under and be squashed by Hemingway).

Barrie was soon making a good living by writing occasional pieces for London newspapers and magazines. He claimed that it was possible to sit down and earn a few dollars in half-an-hour by writing an instant thousand words on any given subject. He proved this by himself writing and selling such a piece on the subject of a door-knob.

But at the same time he was putting his mother's memories of Kirriemuir into his first book, which was published as *Auld Licht Idylls* when he was just 28 years of age. Thus began what became known eventually as the "Kailyard School" of Scottish writing. It implied fiction about working folk with much dialect interspersed, the whole enlivened by a pawky kind of humor and sweetened by a rather sugary sentiment. (The kailyard is a cabbage patch, and pawky is the kind of deadpan fun in which an early film actor like Buster Keaton specialized: wry wit is a good English term for it.)

But your true Scotsman is not a little man. He is never satisfied with small achievements, and he shares with the Jews a chameleon-like quality of being able to adapt himself to any environment and soon become a lord there.

A city scene in Angus, Scotland, poses the question "Which is best? The old or the new?"

Barrie had no intention of mouldering in a garret as a poor Scottish writer of amusing essays. He wanted a Rolls-Royce and a big house and an international name, in other words, plenty of money.

At that time the stage was the thing, and the Kirriemuir boy had always loved acting and players. He contrived to have his first real novel *The Little Minister* properly dramatized, and, together with *The Professor's Love Story*, it made his name and the beginning of his fortune. He went on to fill the London and New York theatres regularly. He was given a title in 1913 and the prestigious Order of Merit in 1922. He became godfather to that Angus Ogilvy already mentioned, son of the great Earl whose family had so long dominated the village of hovels from which the new nobleman and great writer had emerged.

Alas it was not a perfect success story. Is there ever such a thing? Barrie, for all his great talent and his sensitivity, lacked something. He did not have a really first-class mind; and he contributed only entertainment to the wealth of nations. Something missing in him as a man ruined his marriage and made him a solitary, over-careful old man, who was largely driven into that position by inability to face the facts of life. (As when he sent a hundred copies of a limited edition of his new book to chosen friends and couldn't get over the fact afterwards that scarcely any of them had the grace to write him a proper letter of thanks. What did he expect? He came from tough Kirriemuir and should have known he was dealing with human beings, not nice, tail-wagging dogs.)

But he loved childen to the end, and was a benefactor of children hugely, and his reward was not only the lasting annual success of his great children's play in London, but also the hand-rubbings on the bronze statue of Peter Pan which he gave to Kensington Gardens. Some of the ears of the rabbits on that statue, the ears of glitter-bronze, are nearly worn away by the hands of generations of young wonderers and admirers.

True writers and good readers are professionals whose main interest must always be the beauty of the language. Thus we pause in Kirriemuir partly to remember a man whose great talent enriched the English literature which we love, the literature of all the English-speaking countries.

And, by the way, we may reflect on the curiosity that this enrichment of the language should have been effected by a Scotsman, lowly-bred to speak originally one of the most grotesque of all the dialects of the English language.

For that is the "Doric" as growled and coughed up by the Scottish peasantry. "It's a braw bricht nicht an' a munelicht nicht." So did the ploughman Burns provide texts for the Oxford scholars, and the pawky-speaking Edinburgh loon Walter Scott give our libraries the longest list of novels to be found on any shelf. A much smaller man than all these was Robert Louis Stevenson, who, from Edinburgh again, wrote little books but often in such perfect phrasing that they must still be given to children at school for learning how to write their language.

It was the same when the Polish sea captain Joseph Conrad painstakingly taught himself to concoct English prose and ended by being a model for all the academies.

James Barrie of Kirriemuir was a wonderful master of our tongue, whose sentences are more finely constructed today than those of any living writer. That is why he is so important, in spite of the fact that an entire intellectual generation has so heartily disliked him *as a man*.

Yet it is as a man that he must further interest anyone who wants properly to understand Scotland. Burns was not a true Scot, nor even Scott. Barrie was, and it is possible in the bars of Kirriemuir to this day to discover from people who have subconsciously modeled themselves on his character what is good about the Scot and what is his downfall.

They all love to be talked about as "characters," and they all want to be thought clever, and they are all over-sensitive and too quick to take offence. In most of these things they are extremely similar to the Jewish people, and there might indeed be something in the muchmouthed myth that at least one of the dispersed tribes of Israel ended up in this cold, comparatively safe corner of the ancient world.

Barrie was a typical Scot who could be immensely successful and briefly popular, but lost friends eventually by his combined faults of showing off and taking offence. Moreover he was typically over-quick to abandon his native birthright and to adopt the customs of another people, a brilliant but always basically uneasy adaptation. If he, and so many others like him, had only remained wholly Scottish in Scotland then what a nation they could have built!

In that Kirriemuir bar they will be wise-cracking and displaying their extraordinary peasant learning, and they will be disputing and shouting and eventually hating each other's guts so much that there will be no hope for them.

The most brilliant Scotsman ever was the real-life "Admirable Crichton." We know very little about him, but apparently he came in the second half of the sixteenth century out of the usual humble Scottish beginning to astonish the contemporary world of learning with his prodigious memory and extraordinarily agile brain. At universities in those days they would hold public debates for hours on end and the most successful arguer was the greatest man. James Crichton, the uncouth, lowly Scot, could vanquish anyone in argument, and his scholarship was such that today he would be awarded a dozen doctorates. Then he wrote passable poetry and was an absurdly facile linguist, with such a gift of tongues that he could master a new language in a few days. He was about the cleverest man, in the academic sense, that the world has ever known. But as a Scot he was also an athlete, a swordsman, a person of considerable charm, and, what the stay-at-homes have always liked to condemn most of all, an "adventurer." ("Not quite reliable, you know. Fellow hasn't any background, and if I were you I'd lock up the spoons while he's around.")

Thus, according to legend, he came to Mantua in Italy and set himself up as a professor there. He became, as usual, immensely popular. The Scots nearly always do. One of his pupils was a very typical Italian of those days, Vicenzo di Gonzaga, son of the Duke of Mantua. This boy felt that Crichton's great popularity detracted from his own local renown with the girls, so he set upon the Scotsman in a narrow street with some hired thugs. Crichton kept them brilliantly at bay for a while with his flashing sword, but it was not a film and eventually they ran him through. He was just 22 years of age.

So one speaks to those wits in the Kirriemuir bar and is suitably impressed by them and by the atmosphere of the great Barrie that still hangs heavy on the place, but one knows there is really no hope for them. They suffer from a fatal national defect of character.

All the same there are Scots without compare, who can always beat nearly everyone. The history of warfare is replete with legends of Scottish warriors who not only vanquished several adversaries at once but also completely terrified them. In the 1914–1918 war particularly there were many authenticated occasions when situations were desperate until a single tall and red-polled Highlander advanced towards a cluster of Germans with fixed bayonet and routed them (probably killed them all, each manjack).

Up above Kirriemuir are the first of the true Highland glens, or mountain valleys. It was once like exploring a wild land to proceed up the narrow road by the chatter burn or Prosen river, with purple heather on the smooth and breasted hills around, till only the rather

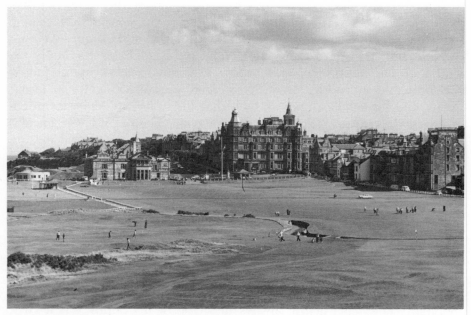

St. Andrews with its golf, its characteristic architecture, and its "guid air."

frightening sound of the solitary curlew bird was company above the noise of an automobile engine, the cessation of whose beat could only mean tragedy.

At the very end of the road, deep in the heart of these ever-darkening mountains, was a small steading or crofter's farm, from which Aberdeen-Angus cattle had come to Perth for the highest prizes and some splendid prices. An American breeder would come wonderingly here and instantly buy a dozen or more females for transportation back to the avid pastures of Virginia.

The farm was, and probably still is, run by a giant of a man, a gentle giant with florid skin and immense hands, and a wife whose charm and looks would have made her one of the most popular of television stars. But she was up with her husband at dawn, and while he was ranging the hills with his shepherd's crook, she would be baking for the palatial teas she would heap on visitors. They had a family of splendid children, among which was one whose infantile malady of a defective heart had nearly broken their hearts. But they had survived and beaten the trouble as the best Scottish folk must.

To visit them from a less successful and well-integrated world was to take a draft from a reviving stream. Life could still be good, even though the snow came in winter and the oats were spoiled and the latest expensive bull refused to work and the English pound was being devalued overnight. This little family was a community and the man and woman running it were, as far as could be allowed, the masters of their destinies. It was obvious that if fortune cast the observer on a desert island or in the front line of a battle he would, with these people at his side, be as certain of surviving as with any companions he might choose from Kamchatka to Tuscaloosa.

The kind of fighting human being represented by this farmer was, of course, to be found in other countries. He would be found among the Samurai-type of Japanese and among some cowboys in what is left of the West, and occasionally in the mountains of Switzerland and in the barracks of Germany, and maybe even in the remoter forests of Sweden still. But he would be an increasingly rare bird, without whom no world would ever get very far.

The road back to Kirriemuir eventually had a signpost "To the Camera Obscura," and here, on a little hill above the smoke of Barrie's "Thrums," was the equivalent of a small public park presented by the great man to the town, with a structure containing that marvellous, typically nineteenth century scientific device, which enabled the visitor suddenly to see, bright in that darkness, all the colored county around.

It was the kind of childish delight that a true Scot like Barrie would just love to give his town.

That is really the best of Angus. Formerly the road would have been taken by the coast, through resorts such as Broughty Ferry, Carnoustie, and old ports such as Arbroath and Montrose. But the resorts have had their day save for the confirmed masochist.

Arbroath has small industries and much sad history, with the ruins of a twelfth century Abbey where once Robert ·the Bruce proclaimed Scotland's short-lived independence of cruel England. Needless to say Walter Scott made much of this place in his novel *The Antiquary*.

The best of Arbroath is the sometimes spectacular seascape. An infuriated, rock coast provides some delightful curiosities of nature, such as caves of stalactites in the cliffs, an arch into the sea which is called the Needle's Eye (probably some shrewd Scots thought they might get into heaven that comparatively easy way), a pile of salt-lashed rocks which a local poet once nicely called the Mermaid's Kirk, a small bay that was once the scene of a romantic and doubtless profitable wreck called the Mariners' Grave, and another rocky device through which the water sometimes spews like steam. It is simply called The Blowhole.

Montrose, up towards the top of Angus, not only continued to inspire Sir Walter (*A Legend of Montrose*) but combines fishing port, light industries and an essentially summer resort quite adequately for the nice old people who come thankfully here each year. The South Esk river expands hugely into a watery basin at the western end of the town. The spirit of the people is shown by two statues in the High Street, one to Hume the philosopher and the other to that Englishman who first made policemen human. He was Sir Robert Peel, and it is because of him that London policemen are still called "Bobbies" among other names.

And they still dispute in this town whether their greatest son was that Joseph Hume or indeed the first Marquis of Montrose. Yes, it was not David Hume but the other "Philosophic Radical," as he liked to call himself, who went out to India as an army surgeon at the end of the eighteenth century and naturally came back with a fortune, but unnaturally spent it on buying a seat in Parliament and campaigning for laws to restrain riches. The Marquis of Montrose was, of course, a more straightforward rebel against England. He was prominent in the unsuccessful Jacobite rising of 1745 and was brusquely hanged in Edinburgh.

Even more representative of Angus than these faded seaside towns is the ancient City of Brechin, encountered on the inland road on the way to the northern border of the county. It has only some 8,000 inhabitants, and no sooner have you entered it than you have left it in a fast car, but it is truly a city by British standards because it has a *cathedral*. Any town in Britain that possesses such a building is by ancient law to be regarded as a metropolis. It shows the kind of hold the Church once had not only on men's imaginations but also on their jurisprudence.

Brechin, if the visitor digs deeply enough (and learns how to call it "Breekin") is very quaint. It is quite unspoilt by tourism or even by its linen, nylon, light engineering and distilling industries. The local people are sufficiently proud of the heavily restored once thirteenth century Cathedral (and of course its Burne-Jones window), and of the remarkable tenth century Round Tower just outside the Cathedral, one of only three of its kind in Britain, which the Celts were apt to build both for protection against their debtors and other enemies and as the most perfect of phallic symbols.

They will also display what they regard as two eminently important birthplaces in Brechin, one of a certain Dr. Guthrie, a nineteenth century divine who was famous for the length of his admired sermons, and the other of that significant modern Robert Watson-Watt, whom the British acclaim as the inventor of radar.

6

ABERDEEN

IT will be found all the time that the smallest hamlet in Scotland is famous not for its cheeses or its automobiles or its popular entertainers who were born there but for its learned men. In most western countries save Scotland and Israel the ordinary people are principally proud of their children if they make money. The Scots and the Jews insist upon their obtaining learning at an early age and their greatest joy is when the child becomes a professor, a minister or a writer.

Thus we proceed northwards from Angus into the small county of Kincardineshire and at the first minute town, Laurencekirk, we are told at once proudly that it was the birthplace of James Beattie and that Thomas Ruddiman worked there, both in the remote eighteenth century. The first was an obscure poet, author of *The Minstrel,* and the second wrote *The Rudiments of Latin.*

Indeed they make much more in Scotland of such worthy scholars than of their more glamorous past. A hill road leads inwards from Laurencekirk to one of the few villages of this country which is as nice as those of England. This is Fettercairn, grouped about a central square, and containing a hotel, the Ramsay Arms, which has never forgotten the fact that it had Queen Victoria and the Prince Consort to stay in 1861. A stone archway across the road will forever proclaim this pride to posterity.

But the much more ancient market cross in the middle of Fettercairn square was originally removed thence from Kincardine itself—and Kincardine is no more.

The site of it may be found if the road back towards Laurencekirk be taken for a short distance and then abandoned at a fork for the Stonehaven road. Pause about a mile along, and on the left, upon Castleton farm, are some ruined stone walls, all that is now left not only of the great Kincardine Castle but also of the prosperous county

St. Machar's Cathedral, Aberdeen, was founded in 1136.

town of Kincardine itself. Where is the town? Where is the busyness and the haggling and the gossip and scenes of young love? Where are the horrors and the intrigues? All gone completely, save for those few ruined stones and the memory as expressed in these words. A similar place is Avenches in Switzerland, once a great Roman city, now just a village and some ruins. Or Sybaris in southern Italy, formerly one of the wealthiest and most pleasure-loving cities in the world. Now the eye can range over what was once these places and see only the triumphant natural beauty of the grass. And it is an affront to the human mind, strangely disturbing.

The kings of Scotland lived in the Castle that dominated the vanished town, but this was over a thousand years ago.

The famous Balliol College in Oxford University was founded by a Norman baron of that name. His son John was a remarkable adventurer who went to Scotland and set himself up as a candidate for the throne. The other candidate was Robert the Bruce. Balliol was actually a stooge for the English, who at first made him Scottish king and then, when he became too self-important, had to march up and depose him. These empty fields are where Edward I of England, "Hammer of the Scots," rode gaudily into a busy town, and, within the Castle, received the surrender of their puppet Baliol (who had in any case already lost one "l" of his name).

Stonehaven is the county town of Kincardineshire today and flourishes in a drab age because it has done little during its history and offers only sands and seascapes and minor resort facilities and a whisky distillery and, in the Town Hall, a collection of etchings. But when Stonehaven says "come and see my etchings" she can, alas, promise nothing more (save the birthplace in nearby Bervie of that John Coutts whose son went to London and founded a famous bank.)

All of which is a very suitable introduction to *Aberdeen*. The unpopulated rural landscapes and the raging, empty coast succumb to modern civilization, here represented by a city of peerless distant appearance from the hills above on an occasional sunny day. It is, like all modern cities, one which sucks the life away from the countryside, but, as the true capital of the north, it is much more than a mere connurbation.

Perhaps that occasional beauty comes first, the product of sun glinting upon the facets of the light-colored granite of which the city is almost wholly and quite uniquely constructed. This granite comes from the Cairngorm Mountains to the west. The architectural style is a nineteenth century mixture of Scottish baronial and eighteenth century old Adam. But occasionally there is the perfect delight of the remote past, as in parts of King's College of 1494 (with the woodcarving in its sixteenth century chapel), and Marischal College, founded 1593 and housed in what must be one of the world's largest granite buildings. This building has, from certain angles, a loveliness beyond compare.

When the misty rain falls, as it must so often, Aberdeen is not so aesthetically satisfying, but another kind of attraction always remains, that of a *unity* in the minds of the men living there. They are wholly interested in achievement, whether it be of the mind or the body; and wherever he goes an Aberdeen man is usually successful at something.

This does not mean, strangely, that Aberdeen has produced a considerable number of men of genius. Far from it. There are much smaller places in Scotland which have contributed far greater men. Aberdeen is like Switzerland in its mentality, aiming at success by hard-work and perseverance. There are several hundred bursaries to the University and each is eagerly taken up by an ambitious, clever youngster from some tiny suburban or village house. In due course the youngsters become very severe and careful teachers, ministers, journalists, doctors and accountants across the wide globe. If true genius cannot flourish in such worthy soil then it is not necessarily deplorable.

Perhaps the greatest man to come partly from Aberdeen was the English poet Byron. His mother was a Gordon of nearby Gight, and eight years of the poet's boyhood were spent at Aberdeen schools. The "gey" Gordons are a strange and wild-strained clan, producing many Byronic men and women.

This is in most weathers a grey and hard part of the world; and a majority of the inhabitants adhere to stern doctrines of moral behaviour, which yield them remarkably rich achievements in an inefficient, wicked world. But there is the inevitable backlash, which produces probably as many illegitimate births in Aberdeenshire as in any other county of the British Isles—and, of course, once in a while, such a genius at least for living and making a lasting name as George Gordon Byron.

He wrote one or two almost perfect English lyrics:

> She walks in beauty, like the night
> Of cloudless climes and starry skies;
> And all that's best of dark and bright
> Meet in her aspect and her eyes:
> Thus mellow'd to that tender light
> Which heaven to gaudy day denies. . .

The immense rest of his output has not always endured, and is often pretentious, prosy and of no importance whatsoever.

But Byron the man will always live, particularly in those countries other than Britain where high-spiritedness is valued far greater than pedestrian worth. Was there ever such a romantic and thoroughly perverse lover before? A lover who came from a town where throughout living history it had been a social crime so much as to whistle a secular tune on Sundays.

At the age of eight he was making passionate love to a little girl named Mary Duff, and when later at 25 he heard that this girl had been married the news, he writes, was "like a thunder-stroke, it nearly choked me, to the horror of my mother, and the astonishment and almost incredulity of everybody."

Apart from Byron it is difficult to think of a really important or supremely noteworthy human being who came from Aberdeen (and of course Byron was only half Scottish). Unless of course it were that original George Keith, fifth Earl Marischal, who founded Marischal College and had carved over a door there the motto which may be translated as "They say? What say they? Let them say."

George Bernard Shaw characteristically adopted this defiant challenge as his own in later days, but it very well expresses always the spirit of your true Aberdonian, a man who makes money out of his own reputation for meanness. They even print in Aberdeen calendars and postcards which make fun of the alleged local parsimony. And of course this is a typical mythology, in that it is the popular expression of something which does not always exist, like the Englishman's belief in his essential reserve and the American's in his native toughness. Aberdonians are not truly careful with money. They can often be a spendthrift lot, and the great financial institutions do not belong there but in much more skinflint Edinburgh.

When the author of this book was a boy of 12 he arrived in Aberdeen early one morning by the London train, and, following his father's instructions, summoned a railway porter to take his baggage to the branch train which he must catch two hours later. He said to the porter shyly "Is there somewhere for breakfast?" The porter led him out of the station and down the harborside to a fish restaurant. The boy groped for the silver coin his father had given him for tipping purposes and presented it to the small, red-haired Aberdonian, who waved it aside, saying "Oh, nae, laddie, it's been a pleasure I'm sure."

The same experience was repeated only once more in a lifetime, and that was in New Zealand, a country of strong Scottish descent.

And the author, whose own ancestors came from this part of hard, mean Scotland, has himself always experienced a deep psychological embarrassment when paying "service" charges on bills or otherwise distributing largesse to menials. He has known in his heart that a truly worthy man should neither accept nor give what is aptly termed a gratuity.

But Aberdeen folk, and nearly all people in the north-east of Scotland are otherwise generous to a fault, once again only equaled by those Jews who have a similar unjust reputation for financial constipation. Almost any Scotsman will be much more generous with his money than almost any Englishman (which is probably one of the reasons why the English have consistently provided the ruling class for the British Isles).

Aberdeen stands on the seacoast and is flanked by golden sands which can be pleasant in good weather. It has several minor industries, including, rather remarkably, that of one of the most successful British antique dealers, but its two hundred thousand-odd inhabitants obtain their livelihoods chiefly from serving the needs of neighboring farmers and from the fishing industry. The discovery of North Sea oil should eventually alter all that.

Glamis Castle, Angus.

Loch Lomond, Stirlingshire.

Edinburgh Castle, Midlothian.

Drummer and Pipers, First Battalion—the Black Watch.

Loch Lomond, Stirlingshire.

Edinburgh. Visitors watching two Gordon Highlanders in West Princes St. Gardens, near Ross Fountain.

The fishing will be properly discussed in a later chapter, but here it may be mentioned that the port of Aberdeen has a rare, romantic flavor, partly the tang of rope and tar and kippered herring, but also the product of sheer size. When the fishing fleet is home it seems that the rows of little ships go on forever and the streets of the port are guttural with rollicking blue-jerseyed men. And the central fish market is the largest in Britain and certainly one of the largest in the world also.

Aberdeen these days, like New York and London and most other cities, is chiefly a place that the traveller cannot avoid, and in which he lingers only for shopping and commercial purposes. But the Scottish city is better than most in that it can be left behind quicker. The road to the nearby Highlands is signposted "Banchory" and swiftly accompanies the pretty river Dee into a valley of green fields and woods of pine and rowan (mountain ash), above which the hills are capped with the purple of the heather.

No one should go to Scotland who finds heather ugly and is depressed by the very sight of it. There are, of course, many such Philistines, and they have something to commend them. A completely

Now all is peaceful at Craigievar Castle, Aberdeenshire.

neutral eye would rightly observe that, save for a short season in the year, heather is a drab blot of tundra-like vegetation which has grown like a disease across what would otherwise be green and pleasant mountains. But for the true Scot, or indeed the compulsive lover of all things Scottish, this plant is as sacred as the asphodel and more beautiful than the flowering cherry of Japan. The prime reason for such idolatry is sentiment induced by historical and personal association. No one who has been in Scotland as a child can ever see the heather again without a tear for remembrance.

But the plant, whether viewed closely through a glass or in the prodigious mass from a great distance, has a subtle loveliness for the aesthetic connoisseur always. Close up, in flower, it is a little bell of beauty; and when it clothes entire mountains and wide stretches of moorland, it can be, in the right mood, a kind of painting done by a pointilliste artist in the most subtle of tones and stippled color. This color is often the true royal purple of the Roman emperors, not modern purple but a pinky, brownish mauve. One true artist only has ever succeeded sometimes in pinning down that beauty permanently for posterity, and he was a nineteenth century English second-rater named Percy. Sometimes the heather-covered mountains of his landscapes are exactly as they appear on a fine day to the wondering tourist or in memory to the sad expatriate.

Thus to proceed up Deeside in the best season of August, and to sniff the woodsmoke from the open cottage doors, and to be startled by the sudden rise of grouse with creaking, umbrella wing from the bee-busy heather above the fine-metalled road is to be transported back to the beauty of the books and the ever-hopeful challenge of childhood:

> The heather in bloom
> Is a carpet laid doon
> O'er ben and o'er brae
> Sae saft to your shoon;
> And the reek in the glen
> Of ingle-nook smoke
> Seems brawly to ken
> My words e'er they're spoke:
> *O haste ye back again to bonny Scotland,*
> *Haste ye back again across the sea,*
> *To folk that lo'e ye best,*
> *Where there's welcome an' there's rest—*
> *O to Scotland haste ye back an' marry me.*

It's all sentiment and in certain ways it's all nonsense, but to those who are tuned-in right—the fortunate ones—it invokes the spirit that moves mountains and the bowels alike.

Banchory (in Kincardineshire) is a resort where quiet people sometimes wisely stay (and visit nearby Crathes Castle, not only for its sixteenth century painted ceilings, but also for its typical gardens of the early eighteenth century).

Up on the right now as the road slowly mounts the valley towards Ballater is the place where Macbeth died. He was an accursed man, doomed like a Hitler or Stalin of his time, but at the end he cried "Lay on, Macduff, And damn'd be him that first cries 'Hold, enough!' " (*Exeunt, fighting. Alarums.*)

Aboyne is a little town that lies in a bed of green nearby; and the fir trees of Cambus O'May further up the road range in color from emerald to malachite. Then Ballater is the railhead and final small town before Balmoral. It stands in a wooded pass, and there is an old bridge across the chatter salmon waters of the Dee. A wise man would stay at the hotel here where bedrooms are lulled by the talking of the stream, and the hallway is decorated with the heads of stags and the stuffed bodies of fabulous fish. Craig-an-Darach is the immense mountain that lowers over all, and it is a smooth mound of heather, just 1,250 feet high. In the Rockies or Switzerland it would go unnoticed but here it is the true monarch of the glen.

Balmoral Castle, up the road to the left, is one of the most remarkable royal residences in the world. None of the European monarchs have left behind such a romantic place; and when an American President concocts such an *idea* he will be suitably immortal. Only the Taj Mahal in India and William Randolph Hearst's San Simeon in California can bear comparison with it as an inspired folly of the regal human soul. It stands on a slight eminence upon the floor of the verdant valley, but is suitably shielded from the main road farther down by discreet conifers. The material used was white local granite which still looks almost as pristine new as the day it was lovingly quarried at Crathie nearby by inspired craftsmen. The architectural design is the purest Scottish baronial of the most Gothic mid-nineteenth century period, and that design was largely the work of one of the best ever of the multifarious German princelings, that Albert the Good, second son of the Duke of Saxe-Coburg-Gotha, who was clever enough to pass high examinations in both the arts and natural sciences at the University of Bonn, and then was married diplomatically to his first cousin, Queen Victoria of England. This marriage, in 1840, was arranged by his uncle, King Leopold I of Belgium.

Probably Albert was the best man ever to sit on an English throne.

What we know as the Victorian age was largely his conception. Victoria herself was the loyal actress who played the parts that he devised; and if he had lived it is possible that Britain might have remained great. As it was the stricken Queen, after her consort's strange death from typhoid in 1861, tried to pursue his wise and high-minded policies, but was at the mercy of her politicians; and the country slowly but surely ran down.

When Albert came to Scotland in the early 1850s he was enraptured

The River Dee, typically seen in winter at Braemar.

by the peace and beauty of Deeside, and bought the old Balmoral estate and had the house completely rebuilt to his specifications, dominating it with a square tower and circular turret rising to 100 feet. It was all done in the two short years 1853–5. How long would it take today? And inside the foreigner provided furnishings that he thought were suitably Scottish, ranging from such tartans as had never been to some of the most extraordinarily ornate tables, chairs and other conveniences ever concocted by northern man. An entire suite was provided of *papier-mâché*, black-japanned and inlaid with mother-of-pearl. It was in doubtful taste but a masterpiece of sheer aesthetic originality.

Each year, when the grouse were ready, the Royal Family would enter their private train (furnished similarly) at King's Cross Station in London and travel joyously to Scotland, where they would do a quick-change act at Balmoral and emerge next morning into that special species of rain known nicely as Scotch mist. They would be dressed as no Highlanders in their right senses would ever have dressed, with feathered bonnets, plaids across the shoulders, kilts discreetly to below the knees, and even thick woollen stockings of the Royal Stewart tartan, and they would carry tall sticks like shepherds' crooks. The amazed peasantry of Ballater and of little Crathie village would greet them with doffed caps and tuggings at forelocks and the small shops of the region would proudly elevate coats-of-arms above their facias after one of the little princes or princesses had come in to buy a happy pennorth of mint humbugs or her Majesty had wonderfully asked to have a new heel put on one of her shoes.

This annual invasion went on for years and continues till the present day, although mitigated somewhat by the innate good sense of present members of that Royal Family. It partook, and partakes, of the nature of a ritual: the wholesale shooting of the feathered grouse, with teams of beaters advancing inexorably to the low skylines; the Sunday morning services at little Crathie Church; the visits of Prime Ministers with well-worn despatch boxes of State documents to be signed; the gracious conversations with foresters and ghillies and grieves and factors (farm managers and estate foremen).

And it is not just a politic method to keep the Scots happy and quiet under their English rule. It is the keeping alive of traditions that never were for the sake of a kind of sheer pleasure each year. Indeed, it might be defined as poetry, of the same genre that inspired Shah Jehan to build the Taj Mahal as a tomb for his most beautiful of wives and the tough Hearst to erect his own kind of Xanadu.

Because when Albert died the plump, desolate little Victoria forever encaged the memory of him at Balmoral in a kind of amber of sad happiness. She had to eschew the tartan in her enduring sorrow and became swiftly an old woman in black, furred with sable and jeweled with jet, who was drawn about the Deeside lanes in a little carriage headed by a shaggy Shetland pony and driven by a faithful retainer, the tall and blunt-spoken John Brown. It is a measure of what has happened to our minds that revelations should now be expected of a sexual relationship between that prudish and mourning Queen and her exceptionally masculine servant. But alas, no evidence can be advanced for this and the reader, for the kind of titillations he wants, must be advised to turn back to *Myra Breckinridge* or indeed to *Paris Match*. Queen Victoria, the woman who was offended if her male children so much as mentioned the legs of the table, had many faults but knew from beginning to end how to behave as one of the last of the great royal personages of the western world.

Braemar, a short distance farther on, is notable chiefly for the annual Highland Games, attended religiously by the Family from Balmoral. Once the clans assembled here were fearsome, and it was the heart of the Scottish matter; but the point of the sword has long since been broken, and what remains is chiefly the kind of British show for foreigners called pageantry. Few peoples have proved so good at this sort of thing, but is it really an art of which the true patriot can be proud? Strutting about in historical costumes and performing ancient rituals is picturesque, but so, so sad; and when local hotel-keepers and ice cream parlors put up their charges for the occasion it can be a positive affront to the true Scottish mentality.

Even the more spectacular of the sports practised at Highland Games have their pathetic side, in that they have long since ceased to be popular save for these special and tourist occasions. When muscular young Highlanders toss the caber (a tapering tree trunk, some 20 feet long, which they can sometimes throw 40 feet) or put the shot (whirling around to reveal that they do indeed wear something under the kilt these depraved days), or when the lassies and the laddies raise their arms and point their patent-leather toes in what remains of the once bloody sword dance, then it is a sorrowful reflection that these are but occasional relics.

The true sport of the modern Scots is Soccer football (which they call "fitbah"); and to observe the true spirit of this people today it is necessary to go not to Braemar but to Hampden Park in Glasgow, especially for a decisive match between Rangers and Celtic. Some 50,000 half-crazed spectators may be present, and often the joyous event ends in real tragedy. (The actual game is a very tame sublimation of the formerly warlike instincts of an emasculated proletariat).

Thus it may be nicer to return to Ballater and thence follow a road left and then left again up through the low and silent hills into the true beauty of old Aberdeenshire. Here the farming, for such a remote clime, is almost perfect. The hay stacks and the drying sheathes of corn in season are arranged not so much with mathematical as with an old maid's precision. Entire slopes can resemble nothing so much as yellow crotchet work. The small black cattle are neat punctuation marks upon the green of other paddocks; and the byres of the low, miniature farm buildings are often cleaner than the bedrooms of

Best of bulls: a Scotch Shorthorn as bred by James Durno of Uppermill, Tarves, of the perfect type that has given the world some of its best beef.

millionaires. (At least the sex there is more normal and infinitely more productive).

On the way, at Tarland, will be passed the great farm enterprises of Douneside, a Trust established by that Lady MacRobert who was one of the last of the true Scottish patriots. Her fortune came from Empire-building and she gave much of it back to the people who made it possible. She also gave her sons, who were among those who sacrificed themselves in the Battle of Britain for the sake of an idea which was soon to be derided by the ungrateful majority.

At Douneside some of the first Highland cattle may be seen, shaggy and with very long horns. They have the virtue of being able to make meat from the poorest pastures, but are chiefly picturesque relics again in a world where only mass production pays.

Just a very few connoisseurs of the best in all things may remember the Aberdeen-Angus bull called Remormon of Douneside, who was in his day a champion of champions, and sired some of the best animals in that breed across the world. He won some twenty championships and nine supreme championships at the most important shows.

Continue to Huntly or Keith and sensibly spend a night or two there, so that this northeast bulge of Scotland, Aberdeenshire, Banffshire, Morayshire and Naira can be properly enjoyed. In few parts of the world are there regions less smeared by progress while retaining the vestiges of what was once a great civilization. It is a delightfully rural area whose rivers rush with salmon and descend to lovely coasts where fish is a fragrant, peasant industry. The climate is strangely un-Scottish, due to some geographical freak. There can be continuous days of sunshine in the early spring, and the soft fruits grow as lushly as in California and with better flavor. The place names are poetically beautiful, from New Pitsligo to Fyvie and from Strichen to the Muir of Fowlis. Craigellachie, Fochabers, Dufftown and the original Dallas compete with Keig and Clatt and Waterton and Echt.

Not only the climate but also the people are outlandish even for Scotland. Most of the original inhabitants, whose descendants are still quite thick on the land, came across the narrow straits from Norway in longboats during the eighth and tenth centuries. They were the last invaders and so settled principally in such exposed coastal regions as these. They are not at all Scottish, these descendants of Vikings, and, lacking both "Celtic" and Saxon blood, they display red hair predominantly and sea-blue eyes. They have long heads and voracious appetites and would rather steal than beg. There is absolutely nothing of the sheep in them, and, perfectionists all, they can frequently go mad with frustration in a regimented world. (Just as their forefathers went suitably berserk.)

They are either farmers or fishermen still (when they are not fighting) and their culture is expressed not in the plastic arts but in oral song and story. Nearly each little place in all this area has a merry legend which can still be recounted by men in bars; and the humor was extraordinarily black long before the more miserable of New Yorkers invented that term. Jokes connected with graveyards frequently affront the quite different English ear, and southerners are similarly afflicted by such tales as that of the man who was frightened by a dog on his way to work each morning and one day kicked it to death.

Such an Englishman, collecting statistics for some absurd social survey, asked about the incidence of divorce in a little Banffshire locality. "Och, we had a wumman who was divorced once," was the reply, "but we staned her oot of toon."

The man who gave this reply wore on his lapel the blue sign to indicate that he had "taken the pledge." He was sworn not to indulge in strong drink. But he habitually carried a flask of malt whiskey in his hip pocket, and, when seen taking gulps from this in suitable hiding places, would explain: "It's for my hairt, ye ken." And, heaven only knew what he would be up to with the very vigorous local girls if he ever got a chance (which his wife would rarely give him). Those local illegitimacy figures owed much to his surface puritanism.

Old Turriff, right in the centre of the great peninsula, has a wonderful story of "the Turra coo," and there was once a miller at Fyvie who did incredible things to his Annie.

At Craigmin there is an ancient double bridge, and of course a local poet must write:—

> Secreted where the rowans rise
> And chasm-deep the burnie plies,
> Twa layers of sepulchral stane
> In Roman archways still maintain
> A royal crossing, and, forbye,
> A refuge where a prince might lie.
>
> Unknown, unlauded, aulder than
> Aught else devised by hand of man,
> More cunning than the greatest feat
> Of modern skill, yet obsolete,
> And hidden—ah, let Craigmin teach
> How human mind can overreach.

The fisher towns and villages of these parts have a way of life which is different from all others, and will be described in a subsequent chapter. Perhaps the most interesting inland town as such is Elgin, capital of Morayshire. It has woollen mills, sawmills, and whiskey distilleries, but the ruined Cathedral goes back to the thirteenth century and there are other historical remains. All the same, a quiet man would not linger there, but might wisely go down to the local port of Lossiemouth, if only to reflect upon the birthplace of that Ramsay MacDonald, illegitimate child of a very poor man, who became Britain's first Socialist Prime Minister—whereupon he adopted the smart ways of London and allowed his hair and moustachios to grow in beautiful wavy locks, and put on knee breeches to go to Court, and eventually sold out completely to the people whom he had been attacking all his life. It is a very sad or amusing story according to taste.

Gordonstoun nearby is one of the most modern and fashionable of great British boarding schools, patronized by Royalty and famous

Best of men: A Highlander at the Braemar Games.

for its usefully spartan way of life. It was founded by a refugee
from Germany named Kurt Hahn.

The excellent river Spey comes down to the sea not far away now
and is one of the best of all for salmon. So plentiful was this fish once
upon a time that the local people got sick of eating it and would rather
have almost anything else, as the people in western lands today tend
to regard the chicken that was formerly such a luxury.

It is good to travel up Speyside through such romantic wooded
scenery as that of Ballindalloch into the country of the Grants, a
family that has produced soldiers and artists and businessmen in sev-

eral continents, but mostly some of the very best Scottish whiskey here. Glenlivet is a bare valley between low and often lowering mountains, and the distilleries are remotely situated where the best soft water comes down. This water hisses into the malt whiskey like soda when poured and a man who quickly quaffs such a highball is walking on air like a human hovercraft soon after.

There are big hotels in Grantown, and there the visitor might be advised to stay rather than in Inverness, which is overcrowded with the contents of long-distance buses. And he might be constrained to run down to such places as Forres, with its further memories of Macbeth, and its two remarkable monoliths outside, one to commemorate

Tossing the caber at a Highland Games.

the periodic burning of witches there in the good old days, and another, over 900 years old, which tells in runic characters for those who can read them how Sweyn of Denmark once defeated Malcolm of Scotland there during his temporarily successful campaign to subdue the British Isles. Or to Culloden Moor, which can be reached by branching off to the left a third of the way along the main road between Nairn and Inverness.

Culloden Moor, as the scene once of a decisive battle in history, is singularly unimpressive. So often the landscape is misted by fine rain; and the Scots have naturally not attempted to make a tourist attraction of their final shame. They had sometimes defeated the hated English in pitched battle but here they were whacked once and for all, and it was left to them only to dominate London in due course as businessmen.

England in the first half of the eighteenth century was much like England today, a nation submerged in sloth and animated only by unpatriotic sentiments of every man for himself, all encouraged by the negative policies of the politician Walpole. She had a small army abroad, which had most unfortunately been placed under the command of William Augustus, Duke of Cumberland, third son of the German King of England. As a result this army was roundly defeated by the French at Fontenoy in 1745—and the second Jacobite Rebellion began.

This was led by Prince Charles Edward, the Young Pretender, a descendant of that Stuart dynasty which had been replaced on the English throne by foreign collaterals, William and Mary, Anne, and then the Hanoverians proper. His father had attempted a similar Scottish uprising against the English in 1715.

His correspondents had told the young man of 25 that England had absolutely no defenses. Its small army was being defeated in Europe. And the Scots would be wholeheartedly behind him if he came over from France to raise the standard of revolt.

He came over in July 1745 and landed not far from where the reader is standing now, upon the empty coast of Inverness-shire. He had just seven men with him.

Within a week "Bonny Prince Charlie" had 2,000 Highlanders marching with him on the road south, and, by the time he came to Edinburgh and entered almost without resistance, there was the final 5,000. That was the most he ever had, but it was enough to go a long, long way, consisting in the main of ferociously-bearded and red-glaring swordsmen of the clans. The Lowland Scots were suitably terrified of these wild men and melted before (but did not really join) them. There was a small battle at Prestonpans near Edinburgh, where a few English soldiers under General Cope and a few canny Lowlanders were soon forced to run by the kilted savages from the north.

Thereafter Prince Charles Edward proceeded in leisurely fashion at the head of his rabble down into England. He took months, obviously preferring to hold sumptuous court in provincial towns rather than to grasp the Hanoverian bull by the horns in London. And he could proceed thus unhindered but slowly through the country because the English Government still had absolutely no army ready to meet him. Walpole, the masterly high priest of inaction, was probably saying "Give the fellow enough rope and he'll hang himself."

And of course Walpole was right. The gallant 5,000 not only became gradually corrupted by unaccustomed good living as they wandered through the lushness of England, but they began to quarrel among themselves. The Macgregors said they should have precedence over the McLeans and the Frasers stopped speaking to the McLeods, and the Gordons were offended by the Forbes. Each clan chief maintained that he only should principally advise the young Prince. These proud wild men were uniformly like that Macneil of Barra whose herald mounted the battlements of his castle after dinner and sounded a horn to proclaim: "The great McNeil of Barra has finished his dinner. The Princes of the Earth may dine now." It was megalomania; it was even magnificent, but it was not really the way to go to war.

When the Highland rabble reached Derby in the center of England they finally broke up into different clan sects and little disputing groups and most of them decided to go back. Anyone who knows Derby can easily understand the motivation of that decision, but possibly the news that the defeated redcoats of Fontenoy had now been brought back to England had something to do with it. The date was December 4 and it was cruel winter after the glorious summer of the original Inverness landing. The clan leaders not only shouted at each other; they dared finally to shout at the Prince. "It's madness, mon, ye ken." And they all turned tail and the retreat began.

By now the English veterans of Dettingen and Fontenoy were marching in relentless formation from London. But they found it difficult to catch up with the Highlanders, who could at least run faster than their enemies. It was not until the two hosts had reached Stirlingshire in Scotland that they made contact. A brief battle was fought at Falkirk—and the Highlanders held the redcoats at bay and even made them retreat, but continued to retreat themselves.

In a kind of animal instinct they made for the true north which was home; and so it was that "Bloody" Cumberland and his disciplined Englishmen finally came up with them at Culloden east of Inverness, where the patient reader continues to stand.

There were still about 5,000 Scots, and their principal weakness apart from their temperament was in artillery. Not only were Prince Charles' guns fewer than and inferior to those of the English but for some typically Scottish reason most of the trained gunners had taken the day off to go to Inverness in search of food (and perhaps women).

The English army consisted of some 9,000 regular troops, and the artillery was particularly modern and well-trained, including the latest type of guns that could fire the devastating grape-shot of that time. This consisted of many small balls put in a bag and fired with a nasty shrapnel effect.

The great battle was typical not only of the age but of all ages. Men do not really want to fight, even when spurred on by commanders who sit safely on horses well out of the firing line, and by skirling bagpipes and infuriating kettle-drums (and fifes from Switzerland).

The two armies remained comparatively motionless within 400 yards of each other on this misty moorland place for over two long hours. No one had the guts to open fire.

Then a characteristic local hailstorm began and the Highland chiefs in particular got restive. They weren't wearing trousers, as yet, and kilts could be a draughty garb. Suddenly the Macintosh of Macintosh gave a wild shout and leapt forward with his broadsword flailing. (It was not for nothing that one of his descendants eventually got really mad and invented the raincoat once and for all).

Those Macintoshes leapt right through the English lines, injuring a few stolid soldiers here and there, but when they reached the end of the thin red lines they were nearly all stone dead. The English infantry had just remained on one knee firing and reloading, firing and reloading, and the poor, reckless clansmen hadn't had a chance.

So it went on. Grape-shot joined the cold rain to infuriate and inspire charge after Highland charge; and the redcoats, when they could kill no more with their cannon and muskets, calmly affixed bayonets and just allowed the wild men to impale themselves upon them.

At the end there were only 50 English dead. But 1,200 Scots were slaughtered in return for those 50, and these comprised most of the heads of the leading clans, and indeed the very flower of a diminutive nation. It was altogether a classic example of military slaughter on a miniature scale, with individual incidents that still inspire the local people to sentimental ramblings. Over a spring that begins a burn or little stream at Culloden is a stone upon which is written "The Well of the Dead." Wounded Scots had crawled to it during the battle for water and one had died with his head in the water. At the end this pool was choked with corpses. The local people, to the present day, will not allow even their cattle to water there. And they have never used the land where so many bodies were buried just beneath the surface. Dig anywhere and bones and bullets will be revealed. Whereas they have grown corn upon a nearby paddock which has another stone, inscribed: "The Field of the English. They were buried here."

Culloden Moor is replete with such inscribed stones, marking places where not only individual clansmen but also the entire clan systems of the Highlands lie forever buried: "Clan Stewart of Appin." "Clan Mackintosh." "Clans McGillivray, MacLean, Maclachlan, Athol Highlanders."

Because afterwards that victorious Duke of Cumberland, now more affectionately known as "Butcher," took decisive steps to make sure that never again should the Scottish Highlands unite. He banned the kilt; he handed over the communal lands to anglophile big families who turned the former free men into breadline tenants; he replaced feudal courts with English laws; and he usefully forced no fewer than 30,000 Highlanders to emigrate to the American colonies long before the American Revolution.

But eventually he got his deserts. He had been proved a military fool at Fontenoy, and he owed Culloden not to his own strategy and tactics but to the reckless folly of the Scots and the wonderful imperturbability of his redcoated Englishmen. At Kloster-Zeven in 1757, during the Seven Years' War of Europe, he was forced to surrender an entire army to the French: and it was his resounding incompetence, indeed, that made it necessary for England to call Pitt to the tribune as an earlier Churchill who might put an end to shame.

"Bonny Prince Charlie?" He wandered a fugitive through the Highlands for five months with a price of some $150,000 on his curly head. Flora Macdonald at one time disguised him as her maid in the Hebrides and rowed him across to the mainland. He had some wonderful adventures before escaping finally to the Briton's last hope ever, which is France (nowadays Spain and Switzerland also) and before degenerating into a hopeless drunkard and a thoroughly dirty old man.

From Culloden on a fine day it is possible to rake with the eye all that salty beauty which is the Moray Firth, and, beyond, to see the strange beckoning loveliness of a maze of land and waterways, the quite unspoiled wildland of the Ross and Cromarty coast. It is necessary to proceed there quickly.

But first, unfortunately, Inverness stands squarely across the land route and cannot be avoided, which is a reason for its great material success as a town. There are communities which make their money the hard way and others which are happier in that they can just sit and take toll.

Everyone who goes to the far north of Scotland must pause if only for half-an-hour in Inverness. Even a big car with filled gas tank would thus be held up in the traffic jams there. And it has been usefully so from the Inverness point of view right through the ages.

Therefore the place should be dodged at all costs. Of course it can be beautiful in certain lights, like all women. The River Ness has some nice bridges and sidewalks. There are shops in the town where tweeds can be bought and deer-stalker caps and the inevitable over-expensive "twin sets." Amateurs of costume jewelry will waste their dollars on "carngorms," huge semi-precious stones from the nearby hills, often set savagely in hairy claws from wild fowl.

The Inverness folk pride themselves on speaking the purest English in the British Isles. It all depends upon what you mean by English. Actually they speak with a pronounced Scottish accent, with that strange foreignness of precision which will be found in the prose of un-English writers of English like Conrad. That diction is really Inverness's chief claim to fame and it is a sufficiently dubious one.

The Castle and the Cathedral are alike over-restored if not downright pastiche, similar to most of the historic remains of truly modern countries like the United States of America and Switzerland. Over-tidy people can seldom display romantic relics from the past.

Possibly the Inverness cemetery on the hill of Tomnahurich is the most interesting single feature of the town. It has a strong Rip van Winkle legend. Two local pipers once played Highland reels for a dance in that boneyard and afterwards they staggered down to the town to find they had been playing for a hundred years and all the architecture and clothing and manners were those of the future. Panic-stricken they sought sanctuary in a church and suddenly crumbled away to dust there.

The recurrence of such legends in different parts of the world evokes the possibility that man can sometimes stumble on holes in the space-time system of the universe.

Thus the true Highlands of Scotland are reached, that region where common sense no longer prevails and the Celtic imagination is all.

7

FISHERFOLK

ALTHOUGH the descendants of Scotland's fisherfolk mostly came
across the North Sea from around Stavanger and Bergen in
Norway, the people absorbed a lot quickly from the "Celtic" aborigines of Scotland whom they killed, raped and enslaved upon these
coastal regions. It will be seen in a moment that their principal culture became just a multiplication of that story from the Inverness
cemetery, nonsense tales of a rare wonder that, alas, could never be.

But whereas upon other European coastlines the Norsemen achieved
great feats of civilization, here upon the northeast bulge of Scotland
they did absolutely nothing at all save continue to submit themselves
to the disciplines of the cruel sea. It was as if something in the climate
and the soil was inhibiting. Not for them the cathedrals and dynasties
which their collaterals erected in Europe. No William the Conqueror
or great Duke of Burgundy or Habsburg family ever arose from the
longboats here. They just put on dark blue jerseys and continued
with the fishing.

The climatic theory for the partial paralysis of human beings on
this bleak coast is undoubtedly the most attractive. Local girls can be
old women by the age of 30. It is all very well to enjoy the mild
blue of the sea and the yellow of the sands on occasional days of the
year, but most of the time, when the visitors are far away, the weather
is as cold and hard as the unlovely grey stones from which the fishing
villages and towns are constructed. The very blood contracts and
men live as in a forced labor camp, fortunate if they can survive. The
fishing is all. There is absolutely no time for anything else, save
connubial pleasures and some Saturday afternoon football.

The strange fishing region begins properly at about Dunbar in the
south, then goes right up round to Inverness, from which it leaps
across briefly to that Ullapool which scoops the western seas. And

there are picturesque but not entirely characteristic offshoots in the Orkney Islands off Caithness.

The most characteristic place of the fisherfolk is right in the middle of the line and is called Fraserburgh. It is a busy little town of solid stone with the characteristic smell of the herring everywhere, and its history is typical of all the principal fishing ports. Throughout the centuries it was nothing much. The fishing was mainly done from what is now the adjoining village of Broadsea. About 1810 there was a miraculous growth, which coincided with the population explosion caused by the Industrial Revolution in England, Europe and America. Ingenious men invented mass production methods of curing the silver herring. A stone harbor was built out into the affronted sea, here, and at others such as Stonehaven, Aberdeen, Peterhead, Banff, Buckie and Lossiemouth. Typical nineteenth century application of science to industry produced specialized boats such as drifters and trawlers to acquire fish wholesale by the most clever methods. Between 1870 and 1900 Fraserburgh and the other ports were metropolises of hard-headed pisiculture. They stank to high heaven but they made money in a big way.

The drifter was the remarkable boat which made much of this affluence possible. It was invented in Aberdeen about 1871, and developed into a long iron craft of some 80 to 90 feet with a tall funnel set well back and a strange brown mizzen sail at the rear. The gross tonnage was 80 to 85 and the engine of some 28 to 33 h.p. would give the ship more than ten knots.

Drifters were immensely seaworthy and needed to be, as the method of their usage was so queer. They shot immense fine nets into the sea. Such a net could be as much as a mile in length, and to own a drifter and its netting was to be a very rich man locally. Most of the boats were owned by syndicates of fairly poor fishermen. Those that had family names, and crests on the funnels (a peculiarly Buckie habit) were the property of families that had almost an aristocratic standing in these small communities.

After shooting the mile of net into the rough sea the plunging steamboat would "drift" with the tide for three or four dangerous hours. Then the great net would be slowly hauled in, formerly by horny hand, then by steam winch. The theory of the fishing is that the herring, being a pelagic species, gathers neatly in enormous shoals not far under the surface of the water. It is not so much caught in the net as caught by it. The fish swim against the wall of fine string and their gills get stuck in the netting. Thousands and thousands of them are eventually and laboriously hauled in, the process often taking hours.

This would just be a matter of hard work if the sea were calm. It very rarely is aught but unpleasantly rough, so the handling of the great nets is a matter for extreme sensitivity of seamanship. As a result probably no men in the world are so skilled in small boats as these fisherfolk of northeast Scotland.

After the huge net has been paid out the drifter is brought round head to wind and the mizzen sail set for its purpose revealed at last: to keep the boat in this required position. Two white lights now show the drifter is fishing, and the lower white light indicates the actual position of the nets.

Each time the drifters came into port they brought thousands of dollars of fish with them, and in the best years of all, between 1900 and 1910, this meant that the cannier of the fishermen aristocrats could make small fortunes. They built themselves fine stone houses in the ports and the softer of their children would leave home to make further fortunes in London and overseas.

The continual bad weather and the rough seas made extraordinary men of these Viking descendants. Consider the aptitudes of those who worked (and still work) with an even more laborious method than that of the drifters. These are the "great-liners," who shoot into the sea some 15 miles of line which is festooned with as many as 5,000 hooks, each of which must be baited separately. But the hard work is unusually rewarded with even more money than the net fishermen get, because the deep-sinking lines catch valuable fish such as halibut.

The really great days of this Scottish fishing industry were over with the First World War, but there have been some spectacular revivals since, notably with the Danish seine-net and new kinds of small boat powered by diesels, based at first on Lossiemouth. And inshore fishermen have in some small places achieved a new prosperity as specialists in the capture of white fish such as the tasty haddock.

In the great days there were, however, principally drifters and trawlers, the last named being strong steam and motor vessels capable of surviving high seas far afield to the very Arctic Circle. Mostly owned by companies, they rewarded the fishermen with shares of the net earnings often, so that a clever and hard working skipper could earn as much as a big business executive in London. In return he had to yield eventually his health or his life, because the voyages were lengthy and unbelievably onerous in the cramped tossing boats. A man would be at least ten days at sea continually and seldom more than two nights at home. And his work would be increasingly complicated by the latest refrigeration plants aboard, so that the catch could be freshly frozen immediately it came out of the swelling sea.

The extent of this industry has never been properly understood elsewhere. In the heyday there were remarkable scenes right down in such English ports as Great Yarmouth, where the herring in particular would be variously cured on a wholesale scale on landing at manufactories in sheds by the harbor jetties. The most delicious method was, and still can be, that known as "kippering," and much of the work was done by small armies of Scottish fisher lassies, who came down to English ports for the purpose in a great annual migration. The tang in the keen air would be something quite out of this world:

> Ah, my juices, what a dish
> Has proceeded from this fish,
> England's joy and Scotia's pride,
> Tanned without but white inside,
> Curving cutely from the pan,
> Hissing still where greases ran
> As a wondrous sea-change fried!

But the Scottish fishing industry suffered its Culloden no less than the nation at large and probably for the same reason. Other causes of this decline have often been given, notably foreign competition and changed habits of eating. But the true cause was more likely the inability of Scots to work together for long as a team. Fishing boats were too often individually owned and the various owners would not unite. There are continual quarrels in village communities all over the world but only in Scotland and places such as Corsica and Sicily are they feuds which everlastingly cut off the nose to spite the face. A Government report on this declining industry once sapiently stated:

> In the main each Scottish boat stands by itself and there is no pooling of results and no possibility of a loss on one boat being balanced by the success of others, as in the case of a company owning a number of vessels. This is mitigated to some extent by the fact that a small number of individuals, mostly on shore, have a share in several boats. The men are also extremely conservative. They are prejudiced against change.

Until quite recently most of the Scottish drifters were so much in debt to fish salesmen ashore that they could scarcely make a living wage for their worker-owners. There has recently been a slow but sure revival in prosperity, which, however, could be finally smashed with the entry of Britain into the European Common Market. Then the better-organized foreigners might come over and elbow the Scots out of their territorial waters.

Which, on the whole, might be a good thing. The Scots themselves would be forced out of one of the hardest ways of life known to man and would undoubtedly do far better for themselves as fishermen no longer but as leaders of the world elsewhere.

So Fraserburgh and the other queer ports may eventually become ghost towns, and as towns in the architectural and urban senses their passing will be unregretted and perhaps even unnoticed. Consider such a place as Buckie, which once had the largest fleet of steam drifters in Scotland and the largest number of resident fishermen. It was absolutely confident that after the First World War its famous prosperity would be revived, and it held on to its old-fashioned drifters when more modern ports had discarded them. But most of those vessels had eventually to be broken-up or otherwise disposed of at a loss. Eventually hardly any herring were landed at the Buckie which had once been the leading metropolis of that finny world. The best of the local fishermen went into seine-net boats and prospered reasonably, but the town was already too large for its truncated income and gradually became little more than a monument to former pride.

Peterhead, between Fraserburgh and Aberdeen, is more fortunate than some of the others in that it possesses both a well-populated prison and a famous canning factory, and it is such a basically hard place that, in some way or other, it should always endure. During the wars, when German prisoners were brought ashore there it was often necessary to brandish guns at the hostile crowds in order to protect those shivering men.

A Buckie man caught a German submarine in the First World War by a typical local device. He had a small gun on his fishing boat and had a wooden structure built around it. When the German submarine surfaced in the North Sea and ordered the fishing boat to surrender this hidden gun was used to blow off the top of the submarine's conning tower, whereat it was the submarine which surrendered. The medal won by the fisherman was not prized because, as he said, it carried no proper financial reward.

Accessory to the fantastic fishing has always been the building of boats. The world as we know it today was largely made possible by people who variously floated trees and set off upon them across dangerous waters. Space craft that now depart for the moon and Mars are only the latest product of such ingenious, northern men. And in the Scottish ports to this day can still be studied how this building was done in its most primitive form. Up in Orkney can be seen, even now, exactly the same "sixerns" and "fourareens" (six-oared and four-oared) craft as originally brought the Vikings over. Fundamentally these first boats, which are still used, were what is known as clinker-built. That is to say they were made of thick planks of fir, overlapping downwards and fastened together with "clinched" nails, then suitably caulked. They rose at the bow and were raked at the stern; and no better design for a boat has occurred to the mind of man since. No other design produces a more seaworthy craft. Many pretty boats have been made for lakes but all of them toss about outrageously in rough seas compared with the Norse originals.

The most common type of fishing boat in the early nineteenth century prior to the introduction of steam power was the "Fifie," a very blunt and businesslike craft that modified the classic design somewhat, having more vertical bows and sterns and eventually the modern method of "carvel" building, which meant that the planks did not overlap but met each other flush. This developed into the famous "Zulu," which was in its day without peer as a primitive fishing boat, sometimes 86 feet long and with tall masts as thick as two feet in diameter at the deck. The brown sails became so large that they could be hoisted only by steam winches. The "Zulus" were the finest fishing craft, as such, ever built by man.

Thereafter the great fleets of drifters and trawlers were steamboat variants of these originals, with iron instead of wood used for the construction, but inevitably the builders went back in hard times to the former methods, and the most common boat eventually was small, luxuriously appointed compared with those of the past, diesel-motored, but still a Viking boat in its methods of construction and design, even to the use of wooden hulls still:

O, build the bonny boatee where the keel runs bright,
With a hammering and a blazing through the cold north night,
And a shaping of the timbers like a whaley on the brae,
And a caulking and a painting that will keep her tight for aye.

O, build the bonny boatee with the cussing and the din,
As Sander shouts his orders and they tease the engine in,
With old Tammas at the rope's end and a Dougal standing tall,
And the diesel in its packing like a wee ane in a shawl.

O, build the bonny boatee till the folk gang frae the toon,
And the Provost's wifey christens her like any mither's loon,
Till Portknockie and Portessie and Portgordon hear the shout
Which announces that anither boat from Jones's yard is out.

But the real attraction of the fishing ports of northeast Scotland

Boats and houses of the fisherfolk.

in a uniform age is their extreme difference from the norm of modern life. The people are so *strange*.

Superficially they are just hard-working peasants of the outmoded kind who have never learnt how to go on strike. They wear drab clothes such as blue fishermen's jerseys and dark trousers and cloth caps. The women can be even less attractive in sartorial appearance. Their little towns are ugly in the grey light; and their societies produce neither great art nor outstanding criminals. Not in two thousand years have these ingrowing communities given birth to a single world-shaker, even of the Al Capone variety, while Leonardo da Vinci could never have flowered in such an alien soil.

All the same there is wonderful material in Lossiemouth and Buckie and Fraserburgh for the right literary artist to mold into a masterpiece one of these days.

Caithness farther north is subtly different from the area that is being described. It has more of the blood and atmosphere of the true Highlands. And probably it was this blood in Neil M. Gunn that encouraged him to write his novel *Morning Tide* over 40 years ago. It is the only one of its class, and describes the life of a Scottish fisher family in some nice prose of the kind that few people can now write:

> The tide was at low ebb and the sea quiet except for a restless seeking among the dark boulders. But though it was the sea after a storm it was still sullen and inclined to smooth and lick itself, like a black dog bent over its paws.

The true fishing ports of the great nineteenth century industrial expansion remain almost wholly undescribed, and could eventually give Scotland one more *Macbeth*.

These are communities which from their earliest days have preferred to intermarry and keep the outside world at bay. Each town and village consists of just two or three families and two or three surnames, which in the course of time have been diversified with "grace" or nicknames for identification purposes. Until quite recently it was almost impossible for a youngster to marry outside the community and especially to bring in a husband or wife from the farming regions a few miles away.

It has been as if they have always been conscious of their foreignness in an alien land and the necessity of sticking together at all costs so that they can remain foreign.

These fisherfolk are still more Norse after more than 1,000 years than Italian communities in the United States are Italian after a brief 50 years.

Of course the fishing towns spew up "sports" from time to time who quite obviously, from an early age, do not belong to the way of life there. But these get out as quickly as they can and never come back. They succeed enormously in other climes but tend to speak with resentment when Scotland is mentioned.

The sensitive visitor can not avoid the feeling here that such a strong spirit of communal living exists as might one day make another militant Israel of these parts. The better kind of expatriate men and money could be attracted back by a social or world cataclysm and a little new nation would be born.

The life of the community is entirely governed and molded by the requirements of the fishing. And this inevitably makes of the community what amounts to a true matriarchy. The men are away at sea most of the time so the towns and villages are essentially in the control of the women.

When the men briefly come back they are pampered like prize bulls. The most menial tasks are done by the women for them. The shoes are cleaned, the boats are scrubbed (or used to be) and above all the miles of net are constantly mended and re-made.

Originally the houses were among the most functional ever, and that was long before Le Corbusier. A part was constructed, often with outside staircase, for the storing of the nets and other equipment. The living quarters were devised like those of a ship; and the double-bed upon which new generations were created and born and old generations died, was hidden discreetly in a recess, closed by curtains or even doors. There were always "kists" or sea-chests for holding clothes; and if all was not spotlessly clean and tidy then the women concerned would be universally spurned and eventually thrown out. Most towns have little settlements outside which are spoken of with loathing and contempt, because they still house the throw-outs.

In the old days the women had to work much harder than was their eventual modern fate. Their duties were specific. They had to assist both in landing and in launching the boats. They even had to carry their husbands aboard, and then bring them ashore on their backs. It was their function to receive the fish when landed and salt it and take it to market or to distant country customers. They bought the food and baked the bread and sought the peat for fuel. In between they bore and reared the children and in every spare moment they were drying or mending the nets.

In modern times women often worry themselves into psychiatric clinics over the ebullience of their children or financial problems, but the wives of the Scottish fishing ports had continually to consider whether they would not be widows tomorrow. They would never be free from the slanting of eyes out towards the lowering sea, and when the fishing fleet came in after a storm there would often be a missing boat. The women would go down to the harbor with their shawls over their heads and would wait.

They were not allowed to show their emotions, and when they went mad, as they often did, it was only in old age. "She's saft-like, ye see, but that's ineevitable at such a grand age." (The grand age in those days would be around 40 or the time of the menopause).

A famous fishwife of these parts would haggle about price as they always did, and her triumphant final line with customers was "Fish are nae fish th'day, they're juist men's lives."

A woman would give birth to a child and be carrying a heavy creel of fish only a few days later. And they were always strong enough to walk as far as thirty miles in five hours or so, carrying fish to market.

In the old days they referred to the natural functions broadly in speech but were rarely licentious. In more modern and Christian times they became outwardly careful but those illegitimacy figures tended to mount.

Finance was, until recently, entirely a feminine affair. The men's job was to catch the fish and endure the seas and the women's was to sell the fish and buy the food and tackle. An investigator writing in the nineteenth century about these parts rather reprovingly stated: "The woman is allowed an influence which in any other condition of life would appear little consistent with either feminine propriety or domestic order. She usually claims the entire proceeds of the white fishing, which lasts ten months of the year, and in addition to baiting her husband's lines, she prepares fish for sale and hawks it around the country."

Some times the men revolted by not going to sea until they were quite sure their wives had absolutely no money left.

The women chewed tobacco and developed leathery skins, but could be attractive in youth. The girls of Buckie were referred to by a writer about 1850 as "handsome, good-looking and the very picture of health."

These girls later in the century became wide travellers, packing their "kists" and departing for distant English ports to earn good money for themselves at gutting, smoking, salting and packing herring. The money they rarely spent but saved for their eventual husbands to use in buying equipment and a share in a boat.

The most important single factor in the lives of these interesting people was and is superstition. But should it really be called that? Our finest intelligences known today have often realized that the laws of chance are the most important in the universe, and if they could be properly understood then life would at last be simple. The great leaders of men throughout history, right down to Winston Churchill, have consulted soothsayers because they have believed that the omens may or may not be propitious, and if they are unpropitious then the best founded enterprise may fail. There are undoubtedly *tendencies,* in cards, weather, economics, politics and in what might seem to be the most haphazard events such as accidents and inspirations. A study of mathematics and the law of averages in particular can sometimes assist a man to avoid the wrong moment for his enterprise—and also a study of old wives' tales and popular superstitions.

The Scottish fisherfolk have tried many kinds of religion in their effort to be efficient and to avoid accidents, but nothing has succeeded so well with them as certain outwardly ridiculous observances in everyday life.

Throughout the centuries sacrifices were made to evil and good spirits alike, especially at the birth of a baby or the launching of a boat. Before boys were allowed to go to sea they had to undergo brutal initiation ceremonies, a crude people's equivalent of modern intelligence and other executive tests. If a boy failed in these he was regarded as no good and relegated to some menial occupation such as shopkeeping—and of course he probably was no good, even if he eventually became a veritable Woolworth of his low profession.

The fisherfolk nearly always married young, in their teens, but chose their partners frequently with the aid of women who had proved themselves as possessing the "second sight." This was and is at least a vestigial ability to foresee the future. There were various methods of divination and a popular one was by the drawing of a straw. The clairvoyant woman would break a straw given her by the young person and draw out a fibre, from which she would predict the color and type of the person whom that young person should marry.

The Buckie fishermen would collect seawater on New Year's Day and sprinkle it over their houses to bring good fortune, but they would never give another man a light from a pipe, and to burn fishbones was almost as unlucky as to admit a cripple to the house. There was a time when valuable nets and lines were destroyed after a person suffering from the "evil foot" had come near them. Some fishermen would always lock doors when attending to their nets, in case the wrong type of visitor should enter. Today they probably identify this same danger with the tax man and take equal precautions. It was considered unlucky also if anyone counted the nets or walked over them.

Boatbuilders liked Friday as a day for laying down a keel, and they would even claim that they could tell from the first stroke of an axe on the keel whether the resultant boat would be lucky. But representatives of the Church would never be allowed near newborn boats, and if a minister so much as walked round the harbor he was thought to be bringing bad luck to the fishing. Similarly cats were not liked, either on the wharves or near the nets and children would be actively encouraged to stone them away.

To ask a fisherman where he was going in his boat was to bring him bad luck. He would curse roundly at the innocent questioner. And one should never, never point towards a boat at sea with out-stretched finger.

Should a boat be wrecked or lose its crew by drowning then no one would ever touch it again, not even the timbers for firewood. (But these could be sold to a neighboring village and then the spell would be broken.)

Three names always brought ill fortune to fishermen, Ross, Anderson and Duffus, and it was very difficult, if possessed of such a name, to get a local job of any kind.

Before a disaster the sea would make strange sounds, emitting "a waichty melody" or "a dead groan."

Certain communities of fishermen actually believed that it was unlucky to rescue a drowning man, and it is a fact that few of the fishermen ever took—or take—the trouble to learn to swim. One of them was once asked why, an intelligent, successful man of considerable education, and he replied: "There's no point in it. It only prolongs the agony of drowning."

Many kinds of fish would never be eaten by these folk because they claimed that they ate human flesh, being found attached to corpses. Nor would eels ever be eaten, because they were supposed to grow from horse-hairs.

In some places it was good luck to go to sea on Sundays and in others it was terrible bad luck.

The poor creatures were forever trying to find a formula for successful living, that was all, and maybe in their superstitious way they were often a little nearer the truth than all the rational sociologists and politicians.

For there is no doubt that if a man encounters more ill fortune than others he is a lesser man, no matter the great extent of his intelligence and talents. It is probably the Jonahs among us that we must most of all seek eventually to breed out.

And that lesson comes not only from the bridge table but also from the bleak and outwardly dull, desperate fishing ports of northeast Scotland.

The luck of the game may well have flowed back temporarily to the fishing towns with the discovery of North Sea oil. The nautical skills of the men are being employed on the maintenance of those remarkable platform-rigs that affront the wild waves between this coast and Norway's. American money manures the rundown fishing ports; and there could be a chill kind of Texas here. Also the final end of a rare indigenous culture.

8

ISLANDS AND
HIGHLANDS

I F the road be taken north from Inverness it will gradually enter
one of the most peaceful and undeveloped areas of the British
Isles. At first there are trees and soggy fields around Beauly, and a
plain run to Dingwall, the proud, minute capital of the broad, empty
county known as Ross and Cromarty. Dingwall still sustains itself
with the thought that "Fighting Mac," otherwise Sir Hector Macdonald, was a native of the burg. He was one of those heroic soldiers
who won and lost the brief British Empire.

Only some 57,000 people inhabit this whole great area of over
3,000 square miles, which has jagged, indented seacoasts on both sides
and predominantly an interior of inspired nothingness. Oh, yes, the
road west can be taken via Strathpeffer, a small resort with the twin
attractions of Ben Wyvis, a 3,429 foot mountain and the "vitrified
fort" of Knockfarrel, to the distant enchantments of Loch Maree, one
of the finest inlets of water in northern Scotland. But whether it will
be worth it will depend upon the weather and the temper.

The narrow roads impose a continual strain upon the driver and can
get into bad condition. Low mountains and beetling landscapes become
monotonous and hotels are very occasional and exert their charms
chiefly upon dedicated fishermen and other confirmed masochists.

If the weather be fair Loch Maree is a beautiful accurate cut
through the black mountains. It reflects back in particular that queer
mass known as the Slioch.

The road from Strathpeffer northwest to Ullapool is even less interesting, and is chiefly known to deep-sea fisherfolk who leave their
ships in that western port and travel back to Lossiemouth and Buckie
and Fraserburgh to spend a necessary night or two with their in-
sistent wives.

Inverness-shire in winter.

A truly adventurous man could and sometimes rather recklessly does continue north from Ullapool, or strikes into the heart of the abandoned land from the east coast farther up. This coast is left at Bonarbridge and the adventure proceeds northwest via Lairg to Lochmore and even to Durness, which is not far from fabled Cape Wrath, the northwesterly tip of Scotland. Now the wanderer will be in the county known as Sutherland. Another road north from Lairg leads to no less a culmination than the place called Tongue.

Here there is a most blessed peace and sombre charm. The sandy bays are empty of all save seabirds and the endless hill pastures know only the lick of strict sheep and the ruminant crunch of long-haired Highland cattle. There is no pollution and neither is there any brisk life. Only the occasional cry of a tax-gatherer can properly disturb a foolish philosopher's dream.

The final county is Caithness. It was chosen by a half-Scottish Queen of England for retirement after her husband George VI's death from lung cancer. The Castle of Mey became her sanctuary. Communities nearby are ingrowing and largely subsistent upon the varied fruits of the sea. Some inland scratchers of the soil actually grow thin crops, particularly oats. (When Dr. Johnson was in the Highlands with Boswell he derided this product as a food fit only for horses, to which the sycophant dared to reply, more or less, "But what horses!")

Belgium has less than twice the land area of these three northern counties of Scotland but ten times the population.

Wick, the capital of Caithness, is curiously a younger town than many in the United States of America, having been founded only in 1808 by the British Fisheries Association to provide facilities for the commercial growth in fishing that was soon to take place. There is everything necessary for moderately successful living in these parts, including a baby airport and several thoroughly adult distilleries.

Thurso, farther up and on the actual north coast, has some curious runic ruins as well as the important function of being the marine departure point for the Orkney Islands.

The tourists also travel thence to the most northerly point of the British mainland where they muse by a flagstaff on a mound which marks the site of a house where a man called John O'Groats lived in the sixteenth century. Who was he? What was he? The books are silent (and indeed they have neglected most of this region, which may, of course, commend it all the more to the discerning modern traveler).

The ancients knew them as the Orcades, these Orkney Islands, and the old name has become poetical with age. A definition of poetry might be the gloss that time smears on the everyday. But the islands have always fired the romantic in writers, right down to comparatively recent times. They are separated from each other to the south by a great, partly landlocked expanse of the sea called Scapa Flow, perfectly remote, deep and calm for Britain's main naval base in the First World War. And it was here that the German Grand Fleet finally steamed in and scuttled itself on June 21, 1919. There never was such a mighty surrender of floating hardware in all history, nor such a waste of money. Scotland, as the operative part of Britain in that instance, had won its greatest victory.

The Romans placed Ultima Thule in these parts, after hardy expeditions of their truly intrepid sailors had ventured around the northern coast of Scotland. And Thule was to them a concept which meant the end of the world and the beginning of the impenetrable unknown, as we regard the black pits of deep space beyond the observable stars today.

The Roman historian Tacitus wrote that the explorers in their triremes (boats with three banks of slave-propelled oars, at which 170 men sweatingly heaved) found that the seas hereabouts were strangely "sluggish." They sensed that they were in magical waters, and fear stopped them from going farther north.

But what they actually experienced was the curious effect of the Gulf Stream Drift upon the sea area of the Orkney Islands. This comes right up from the warm Gulf of Mexico and makes the climate comparatively mild. The main island of the group was and is called Pomona, which obviously derives from the Latin for a place of fruit. It is possible to be warmer and more comfortable in the Orkneys, right up in these northern seas, and to have a greater sense of well-being than a thousand miles south in the more populated and popular places. Especially if the wonderful malt whiskey known as "Highland Park" be imbibed at its distillery in little stony Kirkwall, the main town of the islands. If the Romans could be revived and brought to this place again they would undoubtedly exclaim that "Highland Park" was the original nectar of the gods.

Kirkwall contains only some 4,000-odd people, but St. Magnus Cathedral there goes back in part over 800 years.

There are at least 90 islands in this Orkney group, which is separated from the British mainland by the six-mile-wide Pentland Firth. The eastern entrance to Scapa Flow, below Pomona, the main island, is artificially closed by a remarkable causeway, a built-up road across the sea that uses islands as stepping-stones. This was built in the Second World War as a protection for the Fleet, and, being built at a time of secrecy, is scarcely known to the world at large. To drive along the road which surmounts the causeway is a delectable experience in all weathers. The sea is so near and the low shapes of an island world move mysteriously around the windows of the car.

The main inhabited islands of the Orkneys are Pomona, the Ronaldsays, Hoy, Rousay, Stronsay, Westray, Shapinsay, Eday and Sanday. Hoy has a mountain called Ward Hill. It is 1,560 feet high. Some 18,000 people live and work in the Orkneys as very small-scale dirt farmers and as fishermen.

Yet the strange little archipelago has that authentic magic. Why? Certain world places share it. There is the same feeling in parts of Cornwall and in the Grand Canyon of the Colorado and in the islands of Greece and the old city of Rome and upon the well-trodden winding paths up Fujiyama where the cherry blossoms around the old Buddhist temples open eager, pink lips.

Maybe in very remote history the Orkneys were important as New York is today. They were already finished when Harold the Fairhaired of Norway arrived there in 876 and they remained Scandinavian, a part of the Viking kingdom, for 600 years till promised to

Glen Affric.

Forth Road Bridge.

Near Baddengorm, across to Carn Glas Choire, Inverness-shire.

Loch Morlich, Inverness-shire.

Ben Nevis, Inverness-shire.

Loch Lomond, Dungartonshire.

James III of Scotland in 1468 as part of the dowry of Margaret of Denmark, whom he was marrying. This dowry was not paid, so the Scots sailed across the Pentland Firth in 1472 and forcibly annexed the islands, which would thereafter remain forever a dominion of the Scottish and later the British crown.

But the British Isles are still not finished when Orkney is done. Travel northeast across the darkening and ever-swelling sea and first the two rocks known as Fair Isle may with luck be sighted. There are actually inhabitants on Fair Isle and they have given art more than many huge cities have ever contributed, the essentially hideous but originally strange designs of knitted woolen pullovers or jumpers which have today penetrated from this remote point in the northern seas to a hundred lands. This Fair Isle pattern is, of course, a relic of the runic, primitive art of the original Scandinavian conquerors of the northern world.

Fair Isle is about halfway from the Orkneys to the Shetlands, which do at last complete the British story. This time there are no fewer than a 100-odd islands and the rather brutally named Muckle Flugga

Typical Highland cattle as exhibited by Mrs. J. Bowser of Doune.

Scotland's most viable modern industry—aluminium smelting plant at Invergordon.

at the top is the final outpost of our United Kingdom. The most northerly town of the kingdom is Lerwick on the long piece of territory called Mainland; and Fort Charlotte there was built by Oliver Cromwell, a man who was nothing if not thorough when he set about conquering and permanently pacifying a widespread country. The old houses and narrow streets can be suitably photogenic in fine weather.

Yet the Shetlands lack the strange, romantic charisma of the Orkneys, and are chiefly notable for weird designs in woollen goods—most of the "Fair Isle" monstrosities actually come from the northerly island of Unst—and for the breed of sheep that produces the very soft wool, as well as that hardy, miniature breed of horse known as the Shetland Pony.

Also the names are pretty good and made for the word posturings of a latter-day Milton. There is the Moul of Eswick and Yell and Tresta. Sumburgh Roost is below Fitful Head and there are Noss Island and Scalloway, Gruting Voe, Muckle Roe, Papa Stour, Ronas Voe and of course that isolate isle of Foula with its sole place of habitation called Ham.

Shetland itself was originally called Zetland and that is still its official name, derived perhaps from the last letter in the Greek alphabet. Here was the ultimate.

The name Hebrides is similarly romantic. It signifies something delightful and remote, and so these additional islands were in the days when America had not been discovered. Men thought that there was always hope in the Hebrides, as later they transferred their allegiance to Ellis Island.

This new archipelago protects northwest Scotland from the Atlantic in a long chain of sea-rocks clad with poor grass and occupied by a few, ever-struggling animals, including a modicum of human beings. There are two bastions, the outer chiefly comprising Lewis, Harris and the Uists, and the inner consisting chiefly of Skye, although diversified nicely in the south by Rhum and Eigg. But the sum total of all the actual islands in this group is over 500, and only about 100 of them are inhabited. The rest have been losing men and beasts annually as far back as historians can remember, but somehow there are always renewals. Writers go there for inspiration and mad industrialists at-

The Invergordon aluminium plant from another angle.

tempt extraordinary schemes for economic revival. Wars and rumors of them also help, and at this time of writing South Uist is being manured by a guided missile establishment.

The big island of Lewis has a stern little town and fishing port called Stornoway. This possesses one of the most attractive of Victorian-Gothic castles, as well as such a smell of fish as can never be forgotten. Inland the island is a desolate place of peat, but the west coast has some nice fishing villages. The great stones of Callanish go back to the Druids or farther, and Tolstageluish is truly dramatic. It lies between the ocean and a sudden, mysterious lake, the other shore of which rises vertical to the sky.

Stornoway has the cloth merchants who make the real money out of the Harris tweed which is traditionally hand-woven in these parts. The island of Harris farther down is, of course, where the trade originated. Here once again the barren moorlands affront the civil eye; and how nasty, brutish and short life originally was here can be judged by a sight of the "black" houses, stone-based but rising with slabs of peat to conical roofs that recall the similar communities of central Africa. There are absolutely no windows, and, inside, the people would once shelter from the raging storms outside in a medley of sheep, pigs, poultry, men, women and children and a continual, rankling smoke. This smoke deliciously impregnates the true Harris tweed still.

No wonder these crofters continually irrupted upon the world. Modern America would be a far less successful place if it had not been for their continual immigrations. Leaving home for overseas has always been the principal sport of the islanders; and the Hebrides as a whole might be suitably described as a breeding place for migrant birds and men.

Rough textiles such as Harris tweed have been made all over the world but only in the Hebridean islands of Lewis-with-Harris have the weavers possessed the gumption to make big business of it. This they have done thanks to the enterprise of a few leading families, mainly in Stornoway. Such families, like those of the foremost fishermen on Scotland's northeast coast, have possessed an almost aristocratic quality. Anyway they devised methods of standardization for the production of the tweed, registered a trade mark, and even arranged suitable and recurring publicity in London and America. The innate sense of discipline of the islanders enabled them to stick to the standards and not to cheat.

It is curious that any kind of commercial success should have been made by people who, originally, were not interested in it at all. A

An ancient castle and a timeless loch in Scotland's wild Highlands.

traveller to Harris in the early eighteenth century wrote:

> The natives have cows, sheep, barley and oats and live a harmless life being perfectly ignorant of most of the vices which abound in the world. They know nothing of money or gold, having no occasion for either; they covet no wealth, being fully satisfied with food and raiment.

But they knew how to make that raiment superbly, and when the money came, having no real interest in it by tradition, they were able to hoard it usefully. There was plenty of capital for the big industry that Harris tweed now is.

Dear Skye! How would the pop singers of a previous day ever have got on without you! The Skye *Boating Song* ripples in the ears whenever the name of the inner Hebridean island is mentioned. It has the authentic lilt of Highland sadness and is the type song of the genre, equalled only by a few Irish and Jewish and Swiss laments. As said before it is as if the gods bestow upon frustrated small nations this divine gift of tongues in compensation. Or else the "Celts" are just limited by nature to singing about it rather than doing something more positive.

Indeed the trouble with Skye, as with most of the thousand-odd islands that litter the west coast of Scotland, is that they are unlikely to mean much at all to anyone who has not suffered the benefits of a good literary education. The deep reader who arrives by car ferry at Kylerhea across the little piece of water from the mainland starts thinking at once of Dr. Johnson and Boswell and of Bonny Prince

What remains of the Earl's Palace at Kirkwall in the Orkney Islands.

Charlie and Flora Macdonald. The songs begin to surge about in the high fidelity speakers of his mind, and he thinks the thoughts that lie too shallow for tears.

It must be admitted that a man without these disadvantages sees nothing particularly marvellous in the place, nor in most of the other islands for that matter. They look from the distance as land does to the bored mariner, dark hummocks in the water that at least promise the touch of women. Alas, the islands of the Hebrides look no better close-up than they do from a distance, and can offer practically nothing at all in the way of diversification to a lustful traveller, no soaring hotels of concrete that glare benevolently down upon the suntanned bodies of girl-fish in revealing blue pools.

Once there were many salty characters, as constantly described in the eighteenth century books. Those, or their descendants, are now most of them in America (where doubtless they help to amuse visitors to Congress) and in those days people could still talk of the actual Macdonalds who helped the Young Pretender, and of those Macleods whose famous castle of Dunvegan was always avoided by scared villagers at night because of the dreadful events that had occurred there.

But today the native Highlanders who remain are strangely subdued and more interested in their old age pensions from the London Government than in anything connected with the gallant past.

And their scenery, to the man without education or imagination, is wholly without distinction of any kind, unless it be the distinction of extreme dullness.

On most days the sea and the land and the sky are alike steel-grey. The vaunted mountains, which sound so good in the guide-books, are mere pimples of smooth insignificance. They consist of elevated moorlands, and, even in the case of the famous Cuillins, a dark, razor edge range which backbones the southern part of Skye, are so low by the standards of other countries that the visitor merely wonders what all the fuss has been about. Consider that water usually falls from the sky in these parts and it will be understood that a plain man may be excused for wondering why ever he came to such an undistinguished desolation.

But books have made much of this region. Even the extraordinary journey of the fat man Samuel Johnson and the dancing, sycophantic Boswell his biographer around these parts can invest Skye with a veil of romantic nonsense still. There is the house, Armadale, where the two London literary men disputed with their host the uncouth Sir Alexander Macdonald, contemporary Lord of the Isles and kinsman of the Flora Macdonald who had done her best for Charlie. It is amusing to recall still that Johnson said of his hostess Lady Macdonald: "This woman would sink a ninety-gun ship. She is so dull—so heavy." And to remember how the ineffable Boswell recorded this with typical lickspittle glee:

Mr. Johnson called me to his bed-side this morning, and to my astonishment he *took off* Lady Macdonald leaning forward with one hand on each cheek and her mouth open—quite insipidity on a monument grinning at sense and spirit. To see a beauty represented by Mr. Johnson was excessively high. I told him it was a masterpiece and that he must have studied it much. "Ay," said he.

The place where "The Skye Boating Song" started.

Or to recall Boswell's celebrated description of a real Highlander as encountered on the little boat over to the satellite island of Raasay:

> Along with him came, as our pilot, a gentleman whom I had a great desire to see—Malcolm Macleod, one of the Raasay family, celebrated in the year 1745 for his conducting the Prince with fidelity from Raasay to the Laird of Mackinnon's. He was not sixty-two years of age, quite the Highland gentleman; of a stout well-made person, well-proportioned; a manly countenance browned with the weather, but a ruddiness in his cheeks, a good way up which his rough beard extended; a quick lively eye, not fierce in his look, but firm and good-humoured. He had a pair of brogues, tartan hose which came up only near to his knees and left

them bare, a purple kilt, a black waistcoat, a short cloth green coat with gold cord, a large blue bonnet with a gold-thread button. I never saw a figure that was more perfectly a representation of a Highland gentleman. I wished much to have a picture of him just as he was. I found him frank and *polite*, in the true sense of the word.

Then one must recall the supper party at which the most celebrated television personality of his age actually met the outstanding, Jacqueline Kennedy-type of woman. The only fault that Mr. Johnson could find with Flora Macdonald was that "her head was too high dressed." The odd travellers came to Kingsburgh on the main island where Flora then lived, and Johnson later said:

We were entertained with the usual hospitality by Mr. Macdonald and his lady, Flora Macdonald, a name that will be mentioned in history, and if courage and fidelity be virtues, mentioned with honour. She is a woman of middle stature, soft features, gentle manners and elegant presence.

But, alas, Boswell had himself to record on the spot:

My heart was sore to recollect that Kingsburgh had fallen sorely back in his affairs, was under a load of debt, and intended to go to America.

Even so, a rush of blood to the head eventually made Bozzy continue:

How the sea so often appears off the island of Lewis in the Hebrides.

To see Mr. Samuel Johnson lying in Prince Charles's bed in the Isle of Skye in the house of Miss Flora Macdonald struck me with such a group of ideas as it is not easy to describe as the mind perceives them.

And those who continue to believe that the Scots think only of money should note what the shrewd Englishman Johnson wrote on a scrap of paper while in that actual bed. He wrote in Latin *Quantum cedat virtutibus aurum,* which Boswell translated as "With virtue weighed what worthless trash is gold!"

What Johnson was wonderingly referring to was the reward of some 150,000 dollars which had been placed on Prince Charles's head by the English Government, a reward that none of the Highlanders on Skye had ever dared to claim.

Finally it is rewarding to learn that the Macdonalds did indeed emigrate. The scene of Skye may be dour and the trip a disappointment but at least an American can reflect that Carolina once had its attractions. The Macdonalds went there in 1774, and immediately became involved in the War of Independence. Flora's husband and son were taken prisoner and she returned to Skye alone, being attacked by a French privateer on the way. She fought with the sailors and her arm was broken. She died in Skye and her grave can be seen—and she still has descendants in the United States.

The Macleods have been mentioned. Their main seat, Dunvegan Castle, is one of the most spectacular pieces of architecture in the islands. It stands foursquare upon an eminence, with water on three sides, near a village which has a hotel, the lord of all it surveys (which, unfortunately, is not much). It has great straight walls that are crenellated; and all that the old wives' tales ever said comes immediately true to the imaginative.

The castle and the Macleod family are laced with legends like an old bottle of vinegar with malty wisps of growth. One should be recounted—indeed, it always is—because it typifies what must be regarded as the curse of the Celtic Scots. It is the legend of the Fairy Flag of Dunvegan.

This is the oldest inhabited dwelling in Scotland and the Macleods have been here as local rulers for over a thousand years. Once upon a time their eldest son was born and lay in a high turret room while, below, the clansmen were assembled to celebrate his birth. A nurse was sent up to bring him down and found that he was wrapped in a strange flag. She came down with the wrapped child in her arms, doubtless keening, and suddenly sepulchral voices resounded around the cold walls.

The island of Mull is nicely typical of the inner Hebrides.

These voices proclaimed that the flag could be waved only three times and only to save the Macleods in great danger. If it were waved for no good reason there would be tragedy: and specifically the heir would die, the hated Campbells (all Highlanders express an active dislike of this unfortunate family) would be able to acquire Macleod property, and a fox would become a mother in another of the turret rooms. The last event would be the worst, because it would presage the virtual fall of the family: much of the estate would be sold and there would be insufficient Macleods left to row a boat away from the island.

Let us now consider what actually happened. The flag was waved three times during the ensuing centuries. The first time it defeated the Macdonalds, who had come over fighting. They were faced by only a few Macleods but immediately the flag was waved they thought they saw a great host in front of them and they ran.

The second time there was a disease which killed the Macleod cattle. The doctor flag was waved and the disease departed.

The third time, as recently as the end of the eighteenth century, an estate manager of the Macleods named Buchanan either hated the family of his employers or belonged to the age of reason and wanted to demonstrate the folly of ancient superstitions. He got at the flag secretly and waved it.

At that time the family son and heir was a serving naval officer on a ship called H.M.S. Charlotte. This ship was blown up and the heir with it. A part of the Macleod property was soon after sold to Angus Campbell of Esnay.

And finally a tame fox, foolishly given shelter in the castle, became proudly a mother—and thereafter the Macleod fortunes, at Dunvegan, could only be said to decline. Many Macleods from the island sought eminence in several lands but none achieved the highest eminence; and never after that fatal and final flag-waving were there sufficient of them at Dunvegan properly to row the big boat across the loch. A British politician named Iain Macleod was typical of the unfortunate clan. His department supervised the dismantling of the British Empire. He might have led his political party but disputed with another Scotsman in the cabinet and resigned, enabling Edward Heath to be chosen. He became editor of *The Spectator*. Heath put him in charge of Britain's finances when the Conservatives returned to power, and he was acknowledged to have perhaps the best brain in the Government, but suddenly died.

These Highlands and islands have a great store of similar legends. It could, of course, be argued that such superstitions create their own disasters. Once that flag was waved the fearful Macdonalds knew that they were beaten and they ran. The cattle disease was about to depart anyway, as all diseases must after a time. The fox (a tame one) was deliberately brought into the castle by a typical "friend" and when he heard about it the young naval officer knew he must die and perhaps did not take adequate precautions aboard H.M.S. Charlotte. The land was sold to the Campbells because the Macleods knew that destiny had been arranged that way, and not only the Macleods but also all the other governing families of these parts lost their children to emigration and suffered ever-declining fortunes in the nineteenth century. The politician Macleod of modern times was in any case a sick man.

The flag itself can still be inspected in its glass case at Dunvegan. The castle is open to the public on certain days, a matter which should be carefully studied in advance with the help of a travel agency as the place is well worth visiting and contains interesting old furniture and pictures. But the brown piece of silk in the glass case could well be Moorish; and a Macleod once went on a Crusade where he could have taken it as a trophy.

It has been remarked before that the Scots tend to try with their very acute brains to control the vagaries of life by studying trends and incorporating their findings in superstitions. Which should never, never be despised.

The witch doctors of certain African tribes need only tell a healthy man that he is going to die and he obligingly topples over. If you believe, then what you believe comes true.

It may be a final argument for having no beliefs whatsover.

But a thoroughly candid Scotsman must admit that when he has played badly in several rubbers of bridge it is most consoling to go around saying "I am always a victim of bad luck at cards."

Skye is suitably separated from the mainland by a strip of water called the Sound of Sleat. The principal place of habitation in the island is Portree, which consists of a few rows of small, grey-stone houses joined together as if for protection, also an occasional little steamboat in the profound water that always threatens to engulf the town. There are low hills around that, near the port, actually have moustachios of trees.

Portree lived once, when Prince Charlie came there with that impossible price on his head. The local people did not cash in then but they have since. What happened in the middle of the eighteenth century has forever since sustained them.

The diet of islands may be temporarily interrupted now, and the mainland regained, preferably at Mallaig, so that the heart of the Western Highlands can be visited at Fort William (if, despairingly, the reader did not already proceed thence when halted at Inverness).

There are Fort William and Fort Augustus and they started just like towns with similar names in the United States, as military depots for controlling the wild natives of the region.

And one of the most enjoyable tourist experiences in Scotland is to take a boat trip along what is wrongly named the Caledonian Canal, because this is not at all a canal in the conventional sense of the term, but a system of linked waterways and lochs, rather like the St. Lawrence complex in extreme miniature. The best of Scottish mountain scenery can be studied from the smooth deck of an occasional old-fashioned boat, and at one stage, through the Great Glen, there is peaked magnificence on either side. And finally, before Inverness, the "canal" becomes that extraordinary Loch Ness which, in this day and age, has consistently made money out of a monster which has never been seen.

Thus do the Scots possess, almost in extreme, that faculty of man

Loch Ness, with or without monster.

which, wanting the stars, will even go so far as to invent them. We have wanted giants and fairies and submarine monsters, and have never found any but continue to believe wishfully that they *could* be there.

So people have taken photographs of lines of dark ripples on Loch Ness and claimed that they have seen a survivor of primeval times, an immense creature of the ocean depths who somehow or other became landlocked in Ness. They do not explain how and where his ancestors reproduced themselves. But such "sightings" have always made a good newspaper story in the silly season and have brought money to souvenir huts around the Loch and to local hotels.

In former days Fort William and Fort Augustus pacified (sweet word) the Highlands after the Jacobite rebellions. They were helped by a general named Wade who built Roman-type roads in all directions so that soldiery could swiftly march to any trouble spot and do the necessary. There was an efficiency in the English at this early eighteenth century period that had sadly seeped from them at the time of the similar rebellion in the American colonies.

Thus Fort Augustus eventually graduated and became a monastery and Fort William became still more elevated, a little tourist center with some hotels and souvenir shops and a view of Britain's highest mountain, which is Ben Nevis, all of 4,406 feet high. What the dogged walker sees from the top is still better, a forever-retreating vista of hills that the heather makes gaudy like a carpet from old Tiran. There is even a precipice on one side down which a man at the top of his ambition could fall a sheer 1,500 feet without annoying, intervening projections.

And in winter there will even be sufficient snow to accommodate the curious sports that are promoted with patriotic as well as financially-hopeful zeal by those in Scotland who still believe that Scotland could have a Swiss future without the same certainty of sunshine. These sports consist of sliding down the snow upon flat runners of plastic strapped to inordinately expensive boots, and of sex play in decorative canteens afterwards.

More intelligent, perhaps, are the aluminum, chemical and hydro-electrical works of the Fort William area, among the most viable of modern enterprises in Scotland. A visionary visitor might indeed imagine a day when science, going one jump further, controls the climate and brings land-hungry populations back to this wilderness again.

In the small West Highland Museum of Fort William, among other relics of Prince Charlie, is a lock of his hair, and it is sadly golden like a child's.

Down from Fort William the road watches Loch Linnhe, and then turns left and around another Loch Leven to find the fated Glen Coe, scene of the Glencoe Massacre and explanation of why those Campbells are not popular in the Highlands. But, apart from their name on a can of soup, they do possess an indelible claim to fame. It was in Glen Coe, then a smiling tract of agricultural and pastoral countryside, that one of the cruellest acts in British history took place.

The Macdonalds of Glencoe were Catholics and Jacobites, and in 1691 William III of England demanded that all Highland clans should swear an oath of allegiance to him before the year was out. The ruling Macdonald refused to do this for a while, then wisely changed his mind and departed through a snowstorm to Fort William for the worthy purpose. When he arrived there he was told by typical bureaucrats that he had come to the wrong place and should swear the oath in Inveraray a long, long way down the line. It took him too long through the snow. He did not reach distant Inveraray until January

Pitlochry in the Highlands is renowned for its Festival Theatre.

What visitors to Pitlochry see before they go to the Festival Theatre.

6, 1692, but he took the oath before the Sheriff, and the relevant papers were sent to Edinburgh.

In Edinburgh these papers were suppressed and instructions were sent to the Earl of Argyle's regiment in Inverlochy that the Macdonalds had not taken the oath and it was in order to deal with them as the Earl of Argyle might think fit.

The Earl was clan chieftain of the Campbells, who were hereditary enemies of the Macdonalds.

The soldiers marched under Campbell of Glenlyon, who had actually married a Macdonald and therefore hated them all the more.

But on arrival at Glen Coe the Campbell at first accepted the hospitality of the Macdonald in his house. He played cards with him while the soldiery were given whiskey and food in the barns. He went to bed there and wished the old chief a very good night. But had given his soldiers instructions. They were to arise at five o'clock and set upon the Macdonalds in their beds, not just in the chieftain's house but in every habitation throughout the Glen.

The resulting massacre was a classical example of how to exterminate a family with whom you have quarreled. Macdonald was shot through the heart as the old man started up in bed. His wife, violated by the soldiers, died of her sorrow next day. The formerly smiling valley was soon a place of snow daubed with blood and every house was burned to the ground. Only 38 Macdonalds was the actual death-roll, but they comprised the heart of the clan; and when the Campbells rode away they drove before them a stampede of horses, cattle, sheep and goats, the entire pastoral fortune of the region.

It is worth visiting Glencoe to see how no attempt has ever been made since to improve on the desolation there created. It is one of the gloomiest and least prepossessing scenes in the world, and should fortify those who want to make sure that such events may, one day, never occur again.

Yet how to prevent them save by the imposition of a similar rule of law which the English, typically at Glen Coe, imposed on the Scottish Highlands in those bad old days?

At least the English Government instituted an inquiry and the massacre was proclaimed a crime.

And it is still not nice to have the name Campbell in the Highlands. They could have slaughtered all the Macdonalds in open fight. That would not have mattered. Often the Macdonalds had carved them up unmercifully. But they couldn't do that sort of thing to people in their beds after accepting their always warm Highland hospitality.

While in these parts, if the reader really wants to know the dead center of the wildest part of Scotland, he should proceed from Glen Coe down the desolate road to Loch Tulla and thence to Crianlarich (hotel) whence a very secondary highway proceeds via Loch Tay to the big central Scotland main road, down which lies Dunkeld. All the long way there will just be low mountains and sad, elongated waters. The heather comes nearly to the shores of Loch Tay. It is a wonderfully uncivilized and hopeless region and could cure a man from a nervous breakdown better than all the doctors with their pills.

Glen Coe where the Campbells massacred the Macdonalds on behalf of the English.

A particular experience is to stay a night or two at the Birnam Hotel just down past Dunkeld on the east of that otherwise tourist place. Here are the woods which, in fabled *Macbeth*, came so relentlessly to Dunsinane and spelled the bad king's doom. And the hotel is—or was when last visited—a great roomy place with the atmosphere of a Victorian country house. The baths were giant size and the hot water that flowed into them was soft and brown from the peat. Dinner in a great, pitch-pined hall was conducted like a military operation by elderly waitresses in spick-and-span black and white, and, after a day in the Highland air, that meal tasted good. In the lounge of chintz afterwards old ladies with aristocratic manners would exchange reminiscences about children of their once-great families. There was real slumber afterwards in high double beds.

Swiftly down to Crieff from Dunkeld the road amid the pine forests, the rowans and the heather will skirt the stoned and chatter streams. Crieff is a typical little grey-stone town of tartans and tourists. The way west goes via Comrie, similar but smaller, and is lapped by Loch

Earn. We now begin to enter the most toured district of Scotland, the edge of the area known as The Trossachs. Long-distance buses in Edinburgh and Glasgow have advertisement boards that proclaim the almost instant accessibility of this region. It is actually a combination, as in Switzerland and the Grand Canyon complex, of good roads around an area and of hotels and souvenir kiosks that handsomely pay off the operators. In the right weather it can be very beautiful, but no more so than hundreds of lesser known regions throughout this great northern wasteland of Scotland.

After Loch Earn the southern road passes through Balquhidder and what remains of Rob Roy MacGregor, a grave and headstone in the small churchyard. This man, who lived really not so long ago (1671–1734), is part of the explanation for anyone who wants seriously to understand Scotland. A nation's character reveals itself best of all in its myths. Thus England had Robin Hood and America had Jesse James and Switzerland had William Tell.

Rob Roy to the Scot typifies his secret ambition, to rob the rich to help himself and the poor, to elude authority and beat any man in the world in open fight. Of course Walter Scott sanctified the hero

The Firth of Lorne divides Oban from Mull in the Western Highlands.

in a novel and every little Scots lad, at play with a wooden sword, goes galloping around proclaiming "I'm Rob Roy MacGregor ye ken!"

In reality the mountainous Rob was a farmer of this Balquhidder who preferred like Robbie Burns not to work diligently at his plough but like Robbie to make a kind of poetry out of his life: only not the kind of poetry that is written down. Rob Roy wrote his songs and proclaimed his odes with a sword. He would lead nocturnal expeditions against the cattle of southern farms and come away with horned trophies. He would levy the hated blackmail upon all hard-working folk who wanted to live without fighting. He was a great rascal and a thief; and it was a sure sign that the English were losing their grip when he actually got to London and made an exhibition of himself once—and when he finally died at his Balquhidder farm while the family piper played a characteristic lament.

Once the English sent a brave man to capture Rob. This fool was strung up and hanged with a rope. Another breast thumper followed the trail to see what had happened—and ended face down permanently in a river.

Probably what really made the hero, then and now, was that the hairy bandit, after his successful robberies, was generous with the proceeds. He shall ever be remembered and lauded by Scots who like nothing more than a free handout.

The Trossachs are some low mountains in a triangle between four large and a few smaller lakes, chiefly Loch Katrine and Loch Lubnaig. They narrow down eventually to a single wooded glen or valley, that dips finally into small Loch Achray. The indomitable Walter Scott really started it all off with one of his first major literary works, the long poem called *The Lady of the Lake.*

Let us leave it alone and find our way across to the cleaner islands again, which may be rejoined across enormous Loch Linnhe. Thus Mull is at once the second-largest lump of the Inner Hebrides, wind-swept up to Ben More, with one town only and that a little one, Tobermory, beyond which Spanish galleons were once wrecked after the dispersal of the great Armada by storms and by Drake. Skin divers have found real treasure here; and undoubtedly many of the Spaniards came ashore to darken the hair and enliven the temperament of the Western Highlanders.

And at the far end of the Ross of Mull to the south is sweet Iona, one of the nicest islands of all. Why? It is small and the open ocean winds can scour the mists away and brighten the colors of ancient stone and silvery grass and purple heather.

Then Iona is strangely one of the sacred spots of the earth for those who believe that men can profit from religious observances. It was to this rocky pinprick of the land that Columba came with twelve companions from Ireland in the distant year 563. He was an aristocrat of wild Donegal and such a fervent believer in the new religion of Christianity as taught to him in the declining days of Rome that his voyage was wholly without political or economic significance. Thus it changed the world.

On little Iona a monastery was built and from it the young men went forth into Britain and began a significant conversion of the natives from the old pagan ways of life as practised by the Norsemen to the even harder way as proclaimed by the Nazarene. Much of the world's best ideas and laws eventually proceeded from that conversion but also the decline one day of the British as an irresistible, bloodthirsty people (save in a few pockets of the land, such as Northern Ireland, where continually warring cults of non-Christians assailed each other like Vikings to the end).

So Iona is another of the places which should be visited only by those who are well-read and capable of imagining what is no longer there. A believer can experience the true frisson of poetical remembrance even when he surveys the restored monastery which was tastelessly rebuilt in modern times.

In the year 807 Norse pirates arrived and destroyed Columba's original edifice. Benedictines set it up again in 1203 and it became rather significantly the seat of the bishopric of Sodor. The Bishop got a seat in the English House of Lords. It is where they all go. Then the monastery once again fell into ruins until presented by a Campbell to the Church of Scotland, after which it was inevitably restored with the precision of a post office.

Jura to the south is a great bare island with one single stretch of what the early motorists used to call a road, and it has some hillmountains nicely known as the Paps of Jura. Nomenclature is all hereabouts; and if there was never really a race of Celts there is certainly a strange coincidence of names across Europe. The word Jura in the ancient Gaelic tongue means red deer, and so it is found here where the monied stalkers walk, and also as the name of ancient mountains between Switzerland and France where similar parties of people who can afford it to this day hunt the unfortunate and ruminant quadruped.

Islay below becomes more southern and beautiful, with rolling downs and a final district bravely called The Oa.

Then the mainland comes down in an extraordinary peninsula of land called Kintyre, which is one of the prime reasons for great Glas-

Inveraray Castle, headquarters of the Duke of Argyll, chief of the Campbells, in the Western Highlands.

gow and its maritime traditions. Kintyre walls off the rough Atlantic and so shelters the waters on the inland side that they can be used for great fleets and for boat building alike. The nuclear-powered submarines which would spurt destruction at any eastern aggressors against the western world now darkly lurk here—in exactly the same anchorages as were chosen by Roman triremes and Norse longboats nearly 2,000 years before.

The southwesterly point of Kintyre is only a few sea miles from Ireland, whose misty outlines can be discerned on many days; and it will be realized how close the connection has always been between the two countries.

Campbeltown, Royal burgh in Kintyre, could be made the base for an excellent offbeat holiday of gentle exploration—and trips over to that dark and lowering island of Arran which stands between Kintyre and the conurbations of the Clyde.

Arran is one of the spectacular islands of the world. Seen from Ayrshire on the inner Scottish mainland it is a black mountain in the mists of the western sea. Sometimes it appears so close to the eye that the brain might suddenly have used a telephoto lense. Appropriately it contains a Peak of Death, as well as a place called Lamlash and a northerly bulge which is shyly referred to as the Cock of Arran.

The actual mountains of Arran are as low as any in the British Isles, but can appear immense to the unsophisticate. To such a child's eye they are a final fearsomeness, more real in their horror than anything that has been read of the Rockies or Andes or Himalayas. Goatfell, Cir Mhor and the Castles reach the low skies in edges of rocky destruction. There are precipices and plateaus, and uprising glens like gulches of the dead. The island has a road around it and something like a road through the middle. Crofters live in white-walled and orcharded huts and have the prim ways still of a feudal tenantry. They have been subservient for hundreds of years to the family of Montrose at Brodrick Castle, and as a result many of them still seem to exist in a kind of bemused happiness.

Between Kintyre and the inner mainland, up to the notheast, stretch great sounds of water such as Loch Fyne and Loch Long. Inveraray towards the head of Loch Fyne is the ultimate seat of the sad Campbells, who began as Earls of Argyll in 1457 and enjoyed a long career as fence-sitters with prosperous English connections that eventually brought them a dukedom and a royal marriage. The ninth duke, after going to bed legally with Princess Louise, daughter of Queen Victoria, actually became Governor-General of Canada. Later there were even more momentous American connections. It is an old saying in the Highlands that you cannot keep a Campbell down, whatever might have happened at Glen Coe.

Inveraray Castle is suitably romantic in its wet and bleak climate, with State Rooms, armory, tapestries, pictures and souvenirs to take away (which once included pairs of socks in the local tartan).

At the head of Loch Long is Arrochar, entrance to the Argyll National Forest Park, and here it is but a well-trodden step over to Tarbet and Loch Lomond and a sudden, urbanized end to roaming.

9

GALLOWAY AND DUMFRIES

G LASGOW smears the land right down to the town of Ayr and to Lanark in the center. It would not be so bad if it were a prosperous smearing, but everywhere the landscape is sad with industrial installations of an old-fashioned type that already collect nostalgia like cobwebs, and with the hideous hutments of the men who once migrated from Scotland's and Ireland's farms to earn high wages as Victorian factory workers. One day this will be a zone for the collector, who will wander around the disused coal tips and the rusty cranes and the sightless mills and find the same kind of poetry here that former ages dug out of the ruins of Baalbek and ghost towns of the Wild West. But as yet the rot has not gone quite far enough for tears. Renfrewshire, Lanarkshire and much of Ayrshire are just depressingly rundown, like similar districts around New York and Chicago, and most of Belgium and northeastern France. In their heyday they must have been hellish but grand; and now that heyday is over.

But the reader need not repine. He still has a delectable experience before him, perhaps where he least expected to find it at the end of a very mixed Scottish tour.

First he should pass south through Ayr and turn his face resolutely away from Burns' Cottage at Alloway, and take no notice of the man in the bar who said there were further relics of the poet at Kilmarnock and Tarbolton and Mauchline and Maybole. He must take the coast road so as to come eventually to the wonderful emptinesses of the great district known as Galloway—and immediately to explore Culzean Castle.

Actual examples in Scotland of Robert Adam's architectural work are rare. His father and brothers left many notable buildings behind them. Right here in Ayrshire, near Cumnock in the interior, is an excellent mansion that father William Adam built. It is called Dumfries House, an early product of the classical revival. But Culzean Castle was actually designed by the famous son Robert himself in his most lavish castellated style. It is as if a severe classicist had a German fairy tale dream and remembered it in stone. The western sea laps a high and wooded rock with the gorgeous castle on top. The walls are crenellated at times but the windows and chimneys are good, plain eighteenth century and the rooms inside were designed for flunkeys and for routs and for pictures of ancestors leading the eye to high Italianate ceilings.

To turn off the corniche-type secondary road and proceed through the driveway trees into the lush gardens and then suddenly to see this romantic but sensible pile arising is an experience to compensate for all Glasgow and the subsequent acres of Burns nonsense. The place is open to the public daily and contains the kind of antique furniture and works of art that at least look genuine. And finally, on the top floor with a view of one of Scotland's finest seascapes, is the grand apartment that was presented for his use to President Eisenhower, in gratitude: a typically Scottish gesture. This country, like all, has its faults, but it can never be accused of not knowing how to reward and to thank.

The sentimental American will afterwards find a swelling heart to be soothed by a stroll in those almost unique gardens, warmed by a pocket of semi-sub-tropical climate here. The plants are as rare and wonderful as is the entire conception of towering Culzean.

And afterwards, to complete his joy, the visitor can actually spend a civilized night (increasingly rare in any country) at one of the best hotels in all Britain. This is the Turnberry down the road, which could be described as the sort of hotel Conrad Hilton would have created if he had been an Englishman.

Next morning run up an inland road a little to Crossraguel Abbey. The ruins are sparse but give a brief idea of how prosperous this empty countryside must once have been. The neat fields around contain valuable Ayrshire cattle now but little more and soon the great areas of wild Galloway arise.

Galloway is not a county but a geographical appellation like New England to denote an area. It comprises the large lump of which southwest Scotland consists and for the most part is tawny, grass-grown hills, stretching and convoluting like lazy lions of the land, empty, empty, empty. There are few roads; and the villages when they come resemble outposts of civilization. Yet there is none of the fear that proceeds from real mountains and genuine American wastelands. Perhaps the district is most like a New Mexico in miniature, and it breathes the kind of recuperative peace that usually comes only from deserts. The walker can range for miles without encountering more than an occasional rustle bird. There are few trees, no hedgerows; and even the occasional drystone wall is an exception to the rule of complete terrestrial nakedness here.

Of course it was not always so. Ruins and traditions prove that. But it has been so for so long that the land has really gone back to

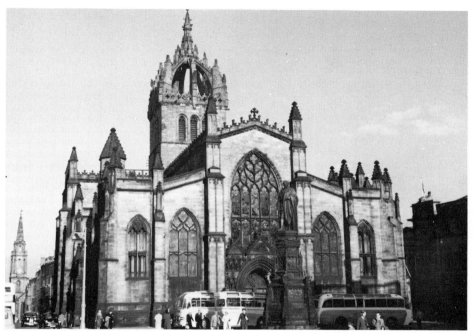

Religious differences have always hurt Scotland but the actual buildings stand firm: this is St. Giles, Edinburgh.

its primitive beginnings and is utterly beautiful to an eye congealed with the blood of cities.

Once upon a time the rustlers and the gangsters ranged here like wild animals; and sometimes what remain of their castles look as if the valleys between the hills have sprouted carious teeth. But the men are gone and not even ghosts haunt their former armored dwellings. For example, the Kennedys. America knows only one such clan, and bases it in Southern Ireland originally. But the Kennedys of Galloway were a tempestuous, utterly irresistible family long before

Columbus sailed. It was written of them:

> 'Twixt Wigtown and the town of Ayr,
> Portpatrick and the Cruives of Cree,
> No man need think for to bide there
> Unless he court with Kennedie.

There were just a few such ruling families, whose names still mean a lot to the comparatively sparse number of human beings who survive in the area. There were the Gordons of Lochinvar. They proceeded on rustling frays from appropriately-named Rusco Castle above Gatehouse of Fleet. There were the MacDowalls who, like the Campbells, profitably sided with the invading English. One of them went to America, and the composer of the *Indian Suite* was a descendant. Similarly the Canadian novelist came from the Maclellans of Barscobe near Balmaclellan. And the Maxwells—how furiously they once rode and reived in Galloway, before the land became too poor for them and they also departed! James Clerk Maxwell was the founder of modern physics, and without his pioneer work there would have been no radio or electronic science.

Frowning above all, the dark Douglases principally terrorized this land in the ancient days. There never was such a clan. Place names all over Scotland recall them, and there are a few in America. To this day one of the most frequent aircraft in which men fly is a Douglas. A history of the family would make one of the most exciting, dramatic, pornographic, bloodthirsty and beautiful books outside of the Holy Bible. But the lovely, empty hills of Galloway are free even of hell-riding Douglases today.

Or Rosses. They came out, the men of Ross, sword-girt from the policies of Balsarroch, right down in the strange Rhinns (which will be described later). They were in their day as wild as the deer which they constantly slew, but eventually they dwindled and they emigrated. Sir John Ross was the early nineteenth century admiral who more or less started the sport of Arctic exploration, and his nephew Sir James R. not only went out with Parry but actually discovered the position of the magnetic North Pole and had Ross Island and the Ross Dependency named after him. A collateral, Sir Ronald Ross, later discovered the malaria parasite and won a Nobel Prize in intervals of writing what might charitably be described as poetry.

But the sweet hills of Galloway have no such dark riders to disturb them today. The men have gone, and where glum settlements remain the principal living objects of real interest are the curious native livestock.

Preeminent among these are the very special Galloway cattle. These beasts are savage in appearance and the most profitable in beef yield from real scrubland. They are black or dun and naturally polled and they will lie out in the winter whatever the weather, being roughly covered with hard skin and hair. They know how to "rustle" as only a Scotsman can, and will help to inherit the world after the next nuclear war. There is also a type of Galloways known as "Belties," because they possess wide belly-bands of white hair. They are small and strange, like the native horse, which is a miniature nag actually mentioned by Shakespeare. These came from the Norwegian ponies landed here by the Vikings. And there were once tiny Galloway sheep, productive of the finest wool, but eventually overwhelmed by the ubiquitous Blackfaced, which became Scotland's answer to the nineteenth century challenge of New Zealand and Australia.

In Victorian times the railroad came to Galloway, but the surviving descendants of the great clan leaders refused to allow it to traverse the narrow coastal fringe of real fertility where their home farms lay. So it had to wander across the remote inland hills and is still a poor little orphan railway there, with depots many miles from the coastal towns it was meant to serve.

The walls begin when those seaside strips are reached and are curiously known as dykes, of which there are two interesting kinds. Where there is sandstone the walls are handmade with neat flat slabs. Mostly, however, Galloway has boulder dykes, just huge irregular stones laid atop each other (with the help of horses drawing wooden sleds originally) and these can be quite indomitable like Roman roads, going up and down steep faces.

Galloway is largely untracked peace save for occasional blots on the more fertile land around the seacoasts. A road runs across the divine wilderness from Girvan on the coast to Newton Stewart down south above an inlet of the Solway Firth. It should be taken, but only by a man who intends to abandon the car at some point and walk regardlessly towards the vacuum hills where they forever rise with the curlew against an illusory horizon.

The best way for others is down an almost equally abandoned coast. Girvan has Kennedy's Pass nearby (where the family would hold wayfarers to ransom) and boats will take the bird-curious over a gentle sea to the immense little island of Ailsa Craig, which is Galapagos-like in its interminable cracks for nesting.

Then there is nothing much till Ballantrae is reached, and indeed Ballantrae is nothing much in itself. But at once the literary mind will arise and snort like a warhorse and not only the beauty of the

The kind of fortress that enabled the former lords of the Lowlands to maintain their sway: Caerlaveroch Castle, Dumfries-shire.

name but also the strangely dulcet air hereabouts will take the sensitive visitor back to childhood and that book read excitingly in bed by the light of an old electric torch: *The Master of Ballantrae*, altogether the Scotsman Robert Louis Stevenson's finest single contribution to juvenile literature forever. Afterwards the road surges inland a little to traverse the sweet wooded valley of Glen App (with the castle remains of one more Family), and comes down south to the

queer inlet of water from the sea called Loch Ryan. It is queer because already the sea waters are becoming sluggish. What has
happened here?

Stranraer at the landlocked end of Loch Ryan receives packet boats
still from Ireland. And the English have obviously made some naval-
military use of the sheltered shores. The sixteenth century Castle
(occupied by the great Graham of Claverhouse in 1682) has gathered
the town of Stranraer around it as an old hen marshals her chicks.
Another Castle, called North-West, was the home of the aforementioned Sir John Ross, the Arctic explorer. Then the smaller houses
of the town are often colored and half-Norwegian or Swedish in
appearance. Old, coaching type hotels could give an indomitable visitor a few days of strange experiences, not the least of which would
be a run down and better still a walk around the remarkable peninsula
or hammerhead into the sea known as The Rhinns. In places it is
only a mile or two wide, with shallow Luce Bay on the mainland side
and the Atlantic Ocean on the other, but throughout it is the most
delectable and peaceful farmland, terminating in a leaping Mull or
headland which rejoices in such a mild climate that palm trees often
grow as in Florida. Port Logan, a fishing village on the so-called
Atlantic coast has half-tropical gardens with plants from the most
distant torrid zones. And the village further boasts a remarkable
fish pond in the rocks, where on a lazy day the wayfarer can lie and
watch the great shadowy forms as they twist wonderingly in the
encompassed water.

The road home west from Stranraer inevitably passes a Castle Kennedy, but then comes to a sweet ruin, that of Glenluce Abbey. In the
thirteenth century this was a monastic settlement, but now only frag-
ments remain of the former magnificence—as of the Castle of Park
upon the hill above, and of Carscreuch where once the *Bride of Lammermoor* lived (no part of Scotland being entirely free of Walter Scott).

The main road should be followed to Newton Stewart, where maybe
a night could be spent. There was once an excellent small inn with
modern conveniences and perhaps it will still be there. The townlet
is unaffected, and the aesthete may like its Tolbooth with the ogee or
double-curved top to the tower.

A side road south should next be followed via Wigtown to Port
William. This Wigtown is nothing. Once the proud center of a rich
county it is now just a drab small place with some unlovely municipal
"improvements." Outside are the Stones of Torhouse, a primeval circle constructed by the mighty men who no longer survive.

Port William scarcely exists—although there was a day when ships harbored here, the place being named importantly at the time after the seventeenth century English king—but when the small road arrives at the decayed settlement then a tour of The Machers can begin.

Here is one more weird, semi-abandoned promontory of the southern Scottish land, a surrounded peninsula with struggle farms and a soft air and the enchanted sea around. This water is normally calmed as if by a magician's spell, and there is the continual feeling that sleeping beauty once again awaits the revivifying embrace of masculinity's prince. Such soil and climate and space *must* know real enterprise again one day.

Silly thoughts inevitably arise from the sheer, temporary peace of the place. Are wars and migrations chiefly caused by vacuums of the kind that crude nature abhors? There is a similar feeling amid the innumerable, half-scratched farmlands of great France. When men overbreed and overcrowd on one part of the world's surface can smiling and fertile emptiness ever long survive? (A few thousand Japanese in this part of Scotland could make it prosperous again in a few years).

The road from Port William skirts the lake-sea for a while and then strikes inland a little to Whithorn, ancient capital of The Machers. It is proudly a Royal Burgh, and it has a population of only a few hundred lost souls. The remains of the Priory Church are inevitably visited; and connoisseurs comment on what was once a Norman door and a seventeenth century arch called "The Pend."

But the actual Isle of Whithorn is all, and of course it is not an island at all, but one more spit of land that impudently protrudes into what remains of the sea. And here will be found a Scandinavian-type village beyond compare in the British Isles. On the map and signposts it is called the Isle of Whithorn, but it is a complete and very ancient village of low white and dark red houses which line the silent waterfront like Viking teeth. Resting tranquil and seemingly forever untouched upon the glass of the tired sea's inlet are open rowboats, properly clinker-built. The climate is softer but the scene is Norwegian or Icelandic. A white church for seafarers actually has its feet in the water (or mud according to the sluggish tides). It is built thus because land was once too expensive in and behind the "town."

The miniature place has a miniature castle, and where the point of the baby peninsula seeks the final sea there is a child's ruin of a very ancient and historic chapel. Here, in the year 397, a local man called Ninian arrived with Christianity for the natives (mainly Picts in those days) and established what was known as a "cell" in a cave. The world was young and Ninian must have enjoyed the same sensations as a social worker from Pekin in darkest Africa these days. The "cell" became a fully-blown oratory after a hundred years, and some nine hundred years after that the swaggering Normans came and they built the chapel whose sparse ruins quietly remind the visitor today that nothing remains but at least something always survives.

One of those boats should be taken and rowed out so that the "Isle" of Whithorn can be seen as a complete artist's picture. It makes a perfect composition.

A thin road from the "Isle" leads northwards along the "sea's" edge to the nothing called Portyerrock and then to what remains of Cruggleton, which is chiefly a real Norman church as repaired privately by a public benefactor. It is one of the most interesting pre-Reformation structures in Scotland, with twelfth century chancel-arch and windows and doors of the original type. Nearby are the ruins of a castle; and indeed such forgotten fortresses could be collected in this little pocket of the land like T. E. Lawrence's crusader castles. There is one at Eggerness up on the right soon, and another before Wigtown, and one over by Loch Machrum to the right. When the land was prosperous it was ruled by those few families in these castles and by priests in the great abbeys of which only those lichened stones remain.

Wigtown Bay is a wide stretch of sluggish tidal water that divides The Machers from the mainland which is Kirkcudbrightshire to the east. (If the reader finds that name difficult he need only remember to pronounce it "Kirkcoodbreesher.") Once again the religious element enters in, because the name is a corruption of the words Chapel of Cuthbert, who was not a P. G. Wodehouse character but a Northumberland shepherd who saw a vision and thereafter travelled as a missionary far and wide throughout primitive Britain in the seventh century. Because he won a reputation for performing miracles and was eventually canonized for it there may be a possibility that he was a pioneer scientist and knew how to bamboozle the peasantry with medical-chemical parlor tricks.

The river Cree mounts estuary-wide from Wigtown Bay into the heart of the silent land and the traveler must skirt lengthily around it, visiting Newton Stewart willy nilly again. When these parts are properly settled in the remote future there will naturally be causeways across all the interfering waters here. But throughout history those wide inlets have divided the land into almost different countries.

The road inland from Newton Stewart mounts into the empty hills again and eventually comes to the heart of the region at New Galloway. This is one more proud Royal Burgh, but, as far back as the records go, has had a population of only a few hundred. It has a railroad depot, a suitable number of empty miles away.

The road from Newton Stewart southeast will be more entertaining. It comes eventually to Gatehouse of Fleet.

This is not only the remnants of glory but also a nice stone village with (at last time of visiting) a sensible hotel.

The glory was in the early years of the nineteenth century, when certain local families deliberately refrained from emigrating and decided to apply the techniques of the Industrial Revolution to the place. Their bet was based on the river Fleet, which would at once drive the huge waterwheels of mills but also admit ships from Fleet Bay to suitable wharves. In a kind of flurry of desperation—because this was the last chance southern Scotland might ever have—the would-be tycoons established cotton mills and a brewery, a tannery, boat-building yards and especially a plant for the manufacture of bobbins (reels or spools for holding thread, as increasingly required around Glasgow and in developing England).

For a very brief space the great family in the mansion house of Cally at the top of the town looked down from their carefully planted woodlands upon the antlike activity of their minions and upon the rising smoke. They sunk mines for lead and copper in the astonished local hills and eventually they even built a gasworks.

But alas it was not viable. Or something happened to the men. The growth was mushroom and suddenly declined as quickly as it had sprung up. Several fortunes were lost and the workers departed for Glasgow or Pittsburgh. Gatehouse of Fleet sank back into the desert quietness from which it had suddenly sprung. The river silted up and the ships remained there briefly as slimed hulks, before becoming wooden skeletons, and finally just green lumps of wood in the wonder water. The gasworks site eventually became that of a garage. The mines became dangerous and brambled holes in the eternal hills.

But you cannot wholly keep a good man down, and the blood of those families survived in one person who eventually made Gatehouse what it now is, quite a prosperous holiday town in miniature. She was the female descendant of local aristocrats, and she developed an old estate into a modern farm, with a prize herd of Galloway cattle. She greatly improved that Murray Arms Hotel, but her supreme stroke of genius was the development of what the British call a caravan site, the revenue from which she ploughed back into other local amenities.

The whinstone houses of Gatehouse, as restored by this prosperity, have a certain dignity, white-painted like dowagers; and the ruins of two castles and of old Anworth Kirk provide a nice local portrait with suitable teeth.

A road eels down by the opened policies of Cally House to reach eventually the only real town and the most beautiful burgh of these parts, which is Kirkcudbright itself. This has been rather ominously described as the Venice of Scotland, and has recently suffered over-much from a daubing of artists. Venice is occasionally recalled when the tide comes up, but otherwise this sluggish inlet of the sea, called Kirkcudbright Bay, can be just an exposed bed of slime. And the artists have never been sufficiently talented to do real justice to the excellent eighteenth century lines of the dour stone houses and their high grouping around the Castle, a brown ruin from the early seventeenth century called Maclellan's House. Some of the houses are brightly painted, and the Tolbooth from the sixteenth century has a spire. Around the town can be traced the Mote (ruined fortifications from a remote past) and nearby the antiquary can visit several similar remains.

Is it worthwhile? Once again all depends upon the visitor's degree of education and imagination. Most readers who honestly examine their minds will admit that nothing is more uninteresting than small ruins of a completely forgotten age. It is a kind of snobbery that leads others on to lengthy side trips and to coldly enthusiastic panegyrics afterwards. Thus we deliberately avoided Cardoness Castle on the way down from Creetown to Gatehouse, and we could have mourned over the ruins of Barholm and Carsluith Castles, also in that area. The big "attraction" down from Kircudbright is Dundrennan Abbey, which consists of a few Romanesque window-frames of stone. Rather more stimulating to the imagination is a farm at Orchardton farther up the road. This supports a curious round tower, of the type which accommodated the fighting families of Ireland and Scotland long before recorded history. It is in its way a fine piece of architecture, and the glinting stones that comprise its rubble-built walls are sufficiently curious.

Now the Vale of Urr is entered, bosky and green, and the hamlet of Palnackie has its intriguing "To the Harbor" sign. Where are the ships and where is the waterfront in this dim region where only the cows float amid pastured mirages of the former water? Eventually part of the river will be found that was once an anchorage for ships that took granite from the quarries of Dalbeattie a few miles away to distant ports indeed. But the mud beneath the reedy water and the mud in men's minds have finally triumphed.

Castle Douglas is now the local metropolis, from which the black clan originally spread out. One of them suitably but not lovingly known to his associates as Archibald the Grim built Threave Castle

The former Marriage Room in the Old Blacksmith's Shop at Gretna Green.

there in the fourteenth century. He was the third Earl of Douglas. A few thousand people cluster in not particularly lovely houses around a little piece of water called Carlingwark Loch today, and their chief joy is a cattle market of considerable local importance.

A wise man in Castle Douglas would either travel up the New Galloway road a little to enjoy the wildness of strangely elongated Loch Ken, or, if interested in stones rather than nature would travel back southeast via Dalbeattie to nicely named Sweetheart Abbey overlooking another inlet of the still and muddied sea, that of the river Nith. Scots with the puritannical type of mind have tried to change the name of this ruin to New Abbey, and today both titles are used but of course Sweetheart is much the best, because the walls are built of an almost pink stone and the remains of window-frames rise in graceful curves. The nave is nearly entire and gives an idea of how great the structure must once have been. It is obvious here that the Scots have always been exposed to much other-worldliness amid their preoccupation with other people's property.

In fact it is only because the subject is now so ineffably wearisome that a considerable part of this book is not devoted to the Kirk and its significance in the Scottish story. It must just be briefly said that those early Christian missionaries who have already been mentioned brought the first degree of civilization to the wilder natives of these parts who had in their turn taken over from an earlier and quite un-traceable civilization. The monks taught the clan leaders some of the Roman arts of living and persuaded the peasantry to drop the more abominable of their pagan rites and to have some consideration occasionally for each other.

But the twin cataclysms of the Reformation and the final English conquest of Scotland turned the churchgoers of Scotland eventually into the most mixed up kind of adult kids. Only in the last Byzantine days of the Roman Empire were there more warring sects than in the Scotland of the eighteenth and nineteenth centuries. The people strangely combined piety with ruthless hatred of each other, and were actually encouraged in this by English politicians who knew that the best way to rule was to divide.

John Knox, a Lowlander from Haddington, started as a priest but forgot his vows when there seemed to be more money in the new Protestantism. In due course he was actually subsidized by the En-glish to stir up dissension in Scotland, and was sent from London for that purpose as Lenin in a later age was sent from Switzerland to the tottering Russia of the Czars. Knox ended, as has been shown before, richly in a fine house of adoring women, an admired tyrant of religion.

He founded the Church of Scotland, aptly named because its func-tion was to destroy Scotland's national character and impose alien habits upon the populace. Here was the initial schism that led ulti-mately to an almost complete fragmentation of the Scots religious-wise.

Consider the Knox-inspired Covenanters of the early seventeenth century. They indiscriminately slaughtered most of their prisoners taken, even women and children. They were just as bad, in their small way, as the greater Nazis in Germany later, or the Russians under Stalin, or some of the more maddened destroyers of Indo-Chinese villages. "Jesus and No Quarter!" was their slogan.

At this present time of writing Scotland, although as ungodly as most other modern nations, has nearly 30 different and mutually ab-horrent denominations of the Christian church. The original splits were often childishly tragic in their basic unimportance. Thus the "Sandemans" featured a "love-meal" of cabbage or kale broth in their services and were known as "Kale Kirkies." But even they succeeded on quarrelling among themselves. An innovator tried out hare in the broth. It was much appreciated by the congregation but somebody pointed out that the Book of Leviticus said the hare was unclean, whereat the hare people broke away in indignation and formed their own church.

In many a small Scottish village, to this day, a person will cross the road and avert his eyes when he sees a neighbor coming who belongs to a different sect.

Enormous disputes and litigations took place between these sects, all conducted in the spirit of an Article passed by the English Parliament in 1921, which blandly stated that the Church of Scotland "as part of the Universal Church wherein the Lord Jesus Christ has appointed a government in the hands of Church office-bearers, receives from Him, its Divine King and head, and from Him alone, the right and power, subject to no civil authority, to legislate and to adjudicate finally, in all matters of doctrine, worship, government and discipline in the Church."

This in spite of the fact that the "established" Church of Scotland actually attracts smaller congregations than the other main denominations.

The ecumenical movement, which means the bringing together of all denominations in one church of Christ eventually, has not enjoyed outstanding success in Scotland. A Glasgow Professor of Systematic Theology wrote a book on ecumenism which contained the significant Scottish words: "I don't think God thinks like these Anglicans. I don't think God is a bloody fool."

That sentence explains a lot—even the recent disastrous "troubles" in Northern Ireland, where the population has a very close affinity to their neighbors the Scots.

From Sweetheart Abbey it is not far to Dumfries and the modern world again. Wigtownshire and Kirkcudbrightshire are sleeping beauties, but Dumfriesshire woke up a long time ago, being continually raped by the traffic over from England. The Act of Union is still appreciated here, because it brought real money. So Dumfries is a busy and prosperous town. It has the most population of any urban area between England and Glasgow—a resounding 30,000 or so, and it contains plants for the manufacture of tweed and hosiery. It is a road and rail junction of importance right through history, as may be demonstrated by the splendid old Devorguilla's Bridge across the broad and smooth flowing river Nith. Remember that John de Balliol, briefly King of Scotland under the English in the thirteenth century. Devorguilla, his widowed mother, must have been a remarkable woman. What feminists do not realize is that there have always been remarkable women. They achieved even more in ancient days than they do now, and they worked by the side of men even more consistently. Anyway, Devorguilla of the difficult name built this Dumfries bridge of local stone as long ago as 1280, and it still stands up strong and stern. (The same woman founded Balliol, one of the best of Oxford University's colleges, and a model for Harvard and Yale).

Dumfries does not, however, attract the sensitive wayfarer as do some of the other places described in this chapter. It has no great beauty and the people tend to live for business alone. The traffic problem of an essentially crossroads town, like that of Inverness, has never been solved. Fumes, noise and parking problems tend to jostle each other.

Even the manifold Burns associations of the place have been over-commercialized, and in the famous Globe Inn the locals will self consciously clown too much for the obvious price of a drink.

All the same, it was on the cold stone step outside the Globe that the foolish poet sat down, "fu' the noo," late one night after a roister session within. And they found him stiff and insensible there the next frosty morning and could only carry him home to his early death.

And the suburb of Maxwelltown, where the braes were once bonny, inevitably recalls home concerts at Edwardian pianofortes and the dulcet, never ending strains of *Annie Laurie*.

Once upon a time Dumfries was a port, and there was a moment when Scotland's only native automobile was briefly manufactured there. (How Scotland has skirted success time and time again but always lost it to others in the long run! How many people know that a principal early architect of the Dodge motor fortunes was Anna Thompson the Scottish piano teacher who married the car man and died at the age of 103 in a palace outside Detroit, leaving over $100 million?)

But Dumfries can teach other lessons. The bookshops are good, thanks partly to the presence in the town of an exceptionally fine Academy. What is that? It is a typical Scottish high school but with a peculiar flavor of its own, akin to that of the French, in that concentration is chiefly on learning. This is the other, better side of the religious medal. The poorest family in Scotland has traditionally sacrificed all for books and fees if it produces a clever child, and usually it does. Should the child be a boy he is destined from the beginning to be a minister, a schoolmaster or a journalist. Rather more money is needed for the more liberal professions, and the doctors and lawyers and accountants do not proceed so often from the whitewashed cottages and the climbing tenements.

These excellent Academies, to be found in most of the towns, have always produced very well educated men and women.

It is only regrettable that they have never concentrated sufficiently on the other aspects of a true education, which England has mastered more thoroughly. What is the use of an encyclopaedic mind if you cannot live in harmony with your fellow men? Scots children are brilliant but rarely acquire what English boys learn on so many metaphorical "playing-fields of Eton." They grow up to bicker and dispute and boast and weep bitter tears of despair. They are most of them like similar over-learned French who know everything save the way to build a stable society.

Away from it all! Because there are hill roads northward from Dumfries without compare. One goes up Nithsdale, and another up Annandale, this last to Beattock Summit, where the long-distance trucks once groaned, and then to Moffat. This is a curious village, formerly a mineral water spa, so that it has some eighteenth century type houses in an amphitheatre of the high ranging and gully striped hills. There is a statue in main street and it suitably commemorates a Blackfaced sheep. From here a man could explore, on foot, the Devil's Beef Tub, traditionally where the rustlers stashed their lowing herds of stolen steers after raids into England, or the source of sweet Ettrick water under Loch Fell, or the ruined castle of Auchen. The Grey Mare's Tail is a spectacular waterfall.

Or another road can be taken from Dumfries northeast to Lockerbie and afterwards up Eskdalemuir. Eventually there is complete silence here, save for the rushing of streams and the occasional music of agile sheep.

Ancient houses and churches and ruins? There are some, but not too many. Maybe the Duke of Buccleuch's mansion of Drumlanrig should be visited. The Scotts of Buccleuch mastered this region long ago and still control it largely. Drumlanrig is one of the best seventeenth century pieces of architecture in Scotland, baronial, renaissance; and it makes a defiant, somewhat over-elaborate bow towards the ever threatening hills.

Or there is the tower of Amisfield near Dumfries, a nice old tower with turrets, redolent of medieval knighthood—or Ruthwell Cross, which symbolizes the ancient fusion of Celtic and Saxon art in these border parts. And Langholm might for some be worth visiting as the birthplace at least of Hugh MacDiarmid, the Dumfries laborer who contrived to be both a Scottish Nationalist and a Marxist in his vernacular verses.

The trip is nearly ended. The southern roads all lead to the Border and Carlisle and it is necessary to stop once only, at Gretna Green.

This was for nearly two centuries the romantic center of Britain. A local blacksmith started the custom of marrying runaway couples cheaply after England decided in 1753 that such clandestine unions should be made illegal. The blacksmith was followed by several other competitive visitors who found this a fine way to fortune; and until recently the place was, for romantics, one of the most important in the world. Alas it became a war casualty in 1940. The "blacksmiths" were finally deprived of their aphrodisiac powers.

But the runaways still go there and what they do is nobody's business. At least they can continue to buy souvenirs. Now that the institution of marriage is a prime object of pollution it is impossible not to pass this gaudy little place without considering what has been lost by those who experience intercourse without tears. (One also mourns for the modern Scot, whose nefarious sources of livelihood have one by one been so truncated by cruel time).

After which the broad mainroad down to England and Carlisle can be a horror indeed.

10

HISTORY

THE most fascinating eras in the history of Scotland are those
about which we have little or no knowledge. This often applies
to the history of any country. But it is not just the fascination of the
unknown. It proceeds from the recent realization of scientific historians that nations like human beings get their patterns forever pro-
gramed in the earliest years of their lives. What Persia was thousands
of years ago so basically she is today, and America, and China and
Russia and Montenegro and Scotland.

If the remote origins of this country be understood then there is
no need to ask questions about her recent behaviour.

Until recently there was a tremendous amount of scholarly controversy about the racial beginnings of the Scots. Savants in the eighteenth and nineteenth centuries disputed on whether they and the
Picts came from Ireland or went to Ireland. The conclusion on which
most agreed was that the origin was "Celtic." Then, in our time, the
younger scholars not only doubted if there ever was a Celtic race but
also if the conception "race" itself should not be finally abandoned.

The present writer believes that the time has come to cut through
all the contradictory words and stick to the known facts. Anyone who
visits Scotland today with open eyes sees basically three kinds of
native people there, the Lowlanders, stolid and round-headed, the
Highlanders, mercurial and long-headed, and the fishermen and
farmers of the northeast coast, as Scandinavian as the Swedes, Danes
and Norwegians.

Right. Now go back to the Roman historian Tacitus, who wrote in
the first century of our era about our country. He almost said exactly
what has just been said about the Scots now. There were to him the
red-haired and large-limbed Caledonians, and the swarthy Silures. He
categorically stated his belief, writing in A.D. 97, that these dark

people descended from Spaniards who had once invaded and occupied the land.

The old Roman historian knew nothing of our modern "Celts," only of "Gauls." In northern Italy, Switzerland, France and what is now called Belgium the Imperial legions met and conquered people of this "race" (if the use of the inevitable four-letter word may be forgiven).

And today the same people clearly give their social and physical characteristics to Switzerland, much of France, much of western Britain. They are, as they were long before Christ, a people with peculiar customs of their own, notably religious and artistic. The pre-historians say now that they originated in the upper Danube basin (very near where other pre-historians say the ancient Greeks originated). Some have called them the basic Arians. And, right back in classical times, they appeared to wondering observers almost exactly like the ideal masculine and feminine types of modern America and Britain: lanky, if possible fair-haired and blue-eyed cowboys with stiff upper lips and a wonderful capacity to be Lone Star Rangers save when consorting with females whose faces came from toothpaste advertisements and bodies out of this world.

The "Celts" of pre-history were, according to the archaeologists, pioneers in the working of iron, and perhaps their most common name eventually became Smith. Then they had an infinite capacity for almost continuous travel. They could not stay in one place long. This brought them into often uncomfortable contact with other peoples. In turn they overran France, Spain, Portugal, northern Italy, and in the fourth century before Christ they had the temerity to descend upon and to sack Rome.

But their inability to stay in one place long was their disability. Being continual overlanders (like so many Americans even to this day) they established no great nations or empires *on their own*, and they never had so much as a capital city.

It is very difficult for the honest modern scholar to disentangle these people from the Greeks, Germans, Russians and Scandinavians of pre-history, save in two respects, religion and art. The "Celts" universally followed the cult known as Druidism. This involved a reverence for trees, especially the oak and its parasite mistletoe (the Golden Bough), and a strange belief in the immortality of the human soul, the last-named enabling them to commit human sacrifices with impunity. Modern religions owe their heavens and hells and their ethical systems to Levantines, but their conception of eternity comes from what the Druids worked out for themselves in the days before books. It is possible that there were, in almost primeval times, the equivalent of oral universities at places in remote Britain such as Anglesey, where thoughtful priests of the tribes, in white robes, got money from the ignorant by telling them that as a reward they would live forever. The extraordinary feature may be that these savages *did* want to live forever.

Then the so-called "Celts" had characteristic art forms, sufficiently different from those of other northern peoples to make them traceable right up Europe to the far north of Scotland. These embraced plainness and simplicity and whorled and strap patterns. It is really the favorite kind of art still in Britain, America, France and Switzerland, if a keen eye looks at the results of design for industry competitions and the shapes of modern automobiles, aircraft and the concrete buildings of our towns.

Tacitus the Roman historian spoke of the Celtic courage in facing danger but cowardice when the danger became overwhelming. Whereas the Romans of the best periods rarely if ever broke, the Gauls nearly always did if pressed hard enough.

At the same time Tacitus shrewdly noted that the "Britons," by whom he meant the people of the non-Celtic parts of Britain, were more like the Romans in their essential tenacity, as indeed they fortunately are to this day.

Then he wrote, more or less: The Celts had noblemen and war chariots, but seldom could their various tribes cooperate together adequately to withstand an enemy. The Roman maxim "divide and rule" was especially exemplified by the successful campaigns against the Celts in France and western and northern Britain. And a heritage of this racial strain in Britain, France and even America still is the so-called democratic system of government, which really consists of eternal quarreling between various parties as to what should be done. Unity comes only in the most extreme crises, and often not even then. Switzerland, a land of Celts originally, is an excellent example of this even at the present day, where not only canton and canton but also commune and commune vie with each other, sometimes against the better interests of the country as a whole. Federalism, with all its faults and virtues, is essentially a Celtic conception in origin.

It is only fanciful to speculate upon the real beginnings of this people, but there are hints here and there to show that maybe they were the remnants of a great civilization, which suffered some cataclysm that pushed the survivors back to savagery but with a few remnants, a few folk-memories of what had once been.

However there was a time, long before the Romans, when the early inhabitants of Scotland resolved themselves into two types of people, the Scots who lived in the mountains and wandered about, tending thin sheep and descending upon their neighbors bloodily whenever they had an opportunity, and the Picts who inhabited the plains and stayed in the one place as farmers, but also liked to make real money from warlike expeditions whenever they had the chance (usually into fat England).

The name Scot in the ancient Celtic tongue more or less means wanderer or vagrant, and the name Pict could similarly mean painted (although these Picts, according to the controversial scholars, were not necessarily Celts at all and spoke a non-Celtic language).

Certainly the Picts, when the Romans discovered them, were a people who liked to strip themselves naked for war like the early Red Indians and paint themselves all over most outrageously. The civilized centurions also liked to think they were cannibals, and maybe they were. Gibbon has a nice note about the habits of the early Caledonians and how they would scour through the woods for an English shepherd and his flock but eat the shepherd rather than the sheep, having a skill at choosing certain juicy parts like the palm of the hand and the feminine breast which is very similar to the primitive gastronomic habits of the Maoris of New Zealand. (Who also painted themselves in strange whorls and near-Celtic patterns).

The Romans called one of these Pictish tribes the Attacotti and defeated them in a battle near what is now Glasgow. A Latin eye-witness wrote down his account of seeing the Attacotti devour their prisoners. The Emperor Valentinian was not, however, really put off, but eventually enlisted survivors of the Attacotti in his own forces and made good soldiers of them.

The Irish like to think that they originally colonized Scotland and gave that country its early tribal kings, but the Scots themselves prefer to argue that Ireland was practically empty before their ancestors went over and established the principal primitive families there. Probably this question can never be settled one way or the other, but some of the earliest Irish tribes of which we have record were of Scottish origin, even the very Erse family of Fingal.

Gibbon believed that the Picts and Scots, after being taught warlike lessons by the first Romans to visit them, went over the narrow water to Ulster and the island they called "Green," which became "Erin" or "Ierne" and "Ireland," whereat they encountered a very squalid and primitive people and swiftly conquered them. The descendants of these invaders (say the Scots) became the native Irish, before they in turn were mastered and diluted by the English. But the Irish say the exact opposite.

It should be added here that students of language classify two main groups of Celtic. The first is the Goidelic or Gaelic tongue, spoken in Scotland, Ireland and the Isle of Man. The second is the Brythonic of Wales, Cornwall, and Brittany in France. (There was once a third division, of the Gallic as spoken in France before Latinization).

To this day there is a deep spiritual cleavage between the native peoples of Scotland and Ireland and of Wales. They are in some ways alike, these peoples, but essentially different, and your true Scotsman, for no particular reason, distrusts and even dislikes a real Welshman from Wales.

Lest the story of Scotland in relation to England might seem to be a wholly one-sided record of nasty colonization from the south and of horrid conquest, it must be emphasized that from the beginning of recorded history the people of Scotland have been predators who asked for it. The Romans would never have trudged up there with their legions if it had not been for the constant raids of the naked and painted Picts into the northern parts of England. Again history demonstrates that history never changes. In the eighteenth century Dr. Johnson teased his biographer Boswell with the remark that a Scotsman's finest prospect was the road to England; and so it was when the Romans were giving England its first real wealth and self-respect, its first modern cities, roads, laws and all of the rest of the human perversities which add up to civilization.

One of the most remarkable men ever to visit Britain was Julius Caesar. Not only did he create the most important and longliving Empire the world has known. Not only was he among the greatest of military commanders. He was also a model for all writers, whose account of his campaigns could not be bettered by the most well-trained of modern journalists.

He wrote of the ancient Britons that they wore their hair long and shaved the whole of their bodies except the head and the usual stiff upper lip. He noted, long before Updike, that wives were shared between groups of ten or twelve men.

But Caesar was sufficiently put off by the climate, and by rebellions in his rear, not to march north. Some ships of his navy must have voyaged in exploration around the Scottish coasts, because he had a good idea of the configuration there and of distances.

In the first century of our era, about a generation after Caesar, Scotland was temporarily conquered (most of the habitable parts) by the great Roman governor Agricola. He marched right up into the Grampian mountains and defeated the wild tribes in a pitched battle. But even Agricola was, like Caesar before him and other Roman leaders after him, quite unable to preserve Scottish conquests. Roads and forts and walls were built. Garrisons were left behind. It was all useless because, for those days, the lines of communication were too long. The Grampian mountains were, logistically speaking, as far from Rome in those days as Indo-China is from Washington in our time: indeed, they were farther away. News and supplies took just too long to reach Rome and the outposts.

After Agricola the Caledonians enjoyed comparative immunity from further attempts to colonize and civilize them for over half a century (during which southern Britain became a rich Roman province) and then Antoninus tried again, ending with a turf wall all the way from Forth to Clyde. But nothing much came of that, and another lifetime passed. Finally the Emperor Severus renovated Hadrian's wall from Tyne to Solway and established forts here and there. For a while he commanded the Lowlands quite effectively.

But in another two hundred years the Romans had finally gone home. They had been in Britain a long time, much longer than empires of the future were to occupy their colonies, but they had to go when they went rotten at the core and wilder peoples became too strong for them on their outskirts. Among these dangerous barbarians were the Picts and Scots of north Britain. They made continual raids south and nearly always returned not only with rich plunder but also with ideas. One by one they subdued the last of the Roman forts and knocked down the walls. The Picts of the Lowlands, in particular, learnt Roman methods of fighting and house-building and even acquired some of their social discipline. Then the Angles and Christianity more or less coincidentally arrived.

The word "Angles" is used only for convenience of historical writing. Once again there is controversy and a deep lack of knowledge. Some scholars describe the barbarians from northeastern Europe who drove the Romans out of Britain as "Nordic," and others as "Germanic." Perhaps it is best to say just that they came from Germany, Denmark, Norway and Sweden and were the first of what romanticists know as the "Viking" hordes, although at this stage they were subtly different from the later invaders who established what we regard as a Norman culture around and throughout Europe.

Scotland was chiefly affected by the so-called "Angles." These were specifically a people of the border country between what are now Denmark and Germany. Modern Hamburg is probably their greatest monument.

Anyway the tradition is that Nordic invaders called "Angles" by subsequent historians came across the sea in longboats and burned and terrorized most of the east coast of Britain right up to the north of Scotland. People on the northeast Scottish coast today are descended from these and subsequent rovers from similar Scandinavian and north German parts. They make the third section of the Scottish nation, after the Highland Scots and the Lowland Picts.

The coming of the Christian religion to Scotland was of equal historic potency. It particularly inspired a clever chieftain named Kenneth MacAlpine to establish the first unity between the Picts and the Scots. He used relics of St. Columba, which he brought to Dunkeld, more or less to give a spiritual basis to the temporary establishment of the first real Scottish kingdom. He was crowned in 844.

Thereafter, for some 150 years, there is a typical dark age of the period. We can guess only at a crude Arthurian regime in this wild north. Little chieftains and precarious kings probably divided their lives between fighting each other with flat swords and contriving robber "quests" on behalf of an increasingly ambitious priesthood. The people remained the same when left alone, scratching the thin soil, breeding animals, killing animals, and casting crude nets into frightening seas.

The true dynasty of Scotland's kings began in 1005 with Malcolm II. Of Malcolm the First little is known. The second king of this name may have been one of the original Scots who realized that the future lay not with the life of the tribe as such but with getting as much as possible out of those southern peoples later to be called the English.

Duncan I succeeded Malcolm, and he was murdered by his chief general, Macbeth (son of Findlaech, a Morayshire chieftain). This in due course gave an English playwright the plot for a sufficiently long-running drama, but also assisted the always difficult unification of an essentially chaotic kingdom. Not only did Macbeth rule well and bring some prosperity to the land, but his sheer audacity brought all the jealous little chieftains together behind Malcolm III, son of Duncan. Eventually the usurper was cornered, by his own superstition as well as the superior forces, and young Malcolm killed him, at Lumphanan.

This Malcolm Canmore, as he was called, became king in 1057 after enjoying the typical education of the better-class Scot then and now. This was an English education, especially diversified in his case by service at the court of King Edward the Confessor. He married twice, and his second bedding was the best, being consummated with that strong-minded Margaret who had been a daughter of Edmund Ironside, then had refused to accept the Norman Conquest of her Saxon aristocracy. She had fled to Scotland with hundreds of other refugees from the iron-mail of France; and when she married Malcolm she persuaded him to enforce as much as possible the anglicization of his country, especially in the south. Then her pious works for the church eventually got her the Oscar of a sainthood from Rome. And when her daughter married Henry I of England it did much to reconcile the old Saxon nobility to the permanence of Norman rule.

All the same her husband Malcolm was from the English point of view a very typical, treacherous Scot. He invaded Northumberland in 1093 and was killed at Alnwick.

They had an excellent son who became King David I of Scotland in 1124, but after the death of Malcolm there had been a kind of obscure interregnum of chieftain kings, Donald Ban, Duncan II, Donald Ban again, Edgar and Alexander I. This is another but brief "dark age," and must have consisted chiefly of clashing claymores (the ancient Scottish long sword, sharpened on both edges for indiscriminate slashing).

David's reign is the most important (1124–1153). He revenged his father's death by invading northern England repeatedly till he had what he wanted in his grasp, all those empty hill-lands that now constitute the permanent border between the two countries. But his aping of Norman feudal customs did not enable him to go permanently further than this wasteland. The south was paralyzed under one of those periodic bad governments that, throughout her history, have prevented England from becoming too successful. This was the government of the wretched King Stephen. David led his valiant Scots time and time again down into England, as far as Durham, even as far as Northallerton. But at the last he was so soundly defeated in the Battle of the Standard, 1138, that he went home almost convinced that Scotland must be completely anglicized or it was lost.

What David did was invite impecunious but well-born Norman knights up to Scotland. He gave them lands and allowed them to build castles. One of these was a man called Bruce and another was a Balliol. It was a very similar process to what went on in the United States of America and Russia after the Second World War, when German rocket scientists were deliberately imported. The rulers of Scotland in David's time and America and Russia in ours realized quite cold-bloodedly that they just did not possess the know-how on their own.

So Scotland was virtually feudalized according to the Norman pattern by David, son of Malcolm and Margaret. In one way it gave the country techniques for civilized living, but in another it established the schism that always existed thereafter, between people and masters. In the religious sense this eventually became a whole series of irremediable splits; and of course the Scots are completely mixed-up to this very day.

William the Lion became king of Scotland in 1165, after the unimportant brief reign of Malcolm IV; and once again here was a partly-wise man who insisted upon imposing typically English institutions upon the land, shires and burghs, magistrates and nobles and vassals. All the good farmlands and fertile coastal strips became little replicas of Normandy in France or Sussex in England. Solely the inaccessible Highlands and the wilds of Galloway retained their ancient Scottish customs and their true tribal chieftains. When the King wanted he could defeat any of them on the plains, using his disciplined and mailclad cavalry against savages who just rushed forward screaming.

But William, however lion-hearted, was sufficiently a Scot himself not to know where to draw the line. Inevitably he also made his invading forays into England—and on one of these was captured and forced to his knees in front of the Plantagenet host. Afterwards the English claimed suzerainty over Scotland, until 1189 when Richard I wisely compounded for an annual cash payment.

There was an Alexander II after William and then an Alexander III, but this last became the final king of Scotland who had in his veins the blood of the true Caledonians. One day his horse carried him right over a clifftop into the always waiting sea and his granddaughter Margaret had to come to the throne. Alas, she never made it. She was the daughter of Eric, King of Norway, and Margaret, daughter of Alexander, a romantic girl known as "The Maid of Norway." Eventually they brought her over but she died in the Orkneys.

Whereupon Edward I of England, pleasantly to be known in the history books as "The Hammer of the Scots," decided that there would be anarchy in the north unless he quickly did something about it. (At the same time he saw his chance of finally constructing a United Kingdom.) He called for candidates to the Scottish throne among the Norman nobles who had been established up there. The most likely were John Balliol and Robert Bruce. Edward opted for Balliol and he was crowned king in 1292.

Edward knew his man. After a few years of being treated as a puppet by distant London this essentially weak individual irrupted, renounced his allegiance to Edward, gathered his forces. But the other Scottish Normans, notably those who supported Bruce, faded away when Edward came.

Balliol was deposed and Edward took over Scotland completely, marching up and down its length and breadth and eventually taking the coronation stone from Scone near Perth to its permanent resting-place thereafter in Westminster. It was the end.

It was not. Edward of England was briefly king of Scotland as well. He technically remained so for ten years, during which military governors acted as military governors must, cruelly in intervals of making money, and the English soldiery had too good a time grabbing not only the produce of the farms but also the girls.

The Scots squirmed, and out of their agony arose the very tall figure of Sir William Wallace.

He was the son of a landed proprietor near Paisley (then divine woodland but now largely a place of Blake's "dark, satanic mills"). And at the age of 25 he became one of the world's first guerrilla leaders of genius.

Although young Wallace's genius was for the hit-and-run, the Robin Hood tactics of the always enveloping woods in those unspoilt days, he stood up to the English twice in pitched battle. The first time was down below the castled hill of Stirling, by a bridge end on the river Forth. He was very lucky. The English commander was typical of the English damned fools who arise toothily from time to time as a product of too much pride and inbreeding. His name was the Earl of Warenne. He deployed his thin forces wrongly and they were overwhelmed by the wild Scots who suddenly descended on them with the gigantic Wallace at their head.

There ensued for a comparatively brief time what still in memory restores the spirits of the Scots when they feel down, a period of truly national upsurgence against a hated foreign occupier. Wallace and his men kept to the woods and mountains as much as possible and gave the English soldiery nightmares. If that soldiery could have got marijuana in those days they would have become addicted to it. The Scots for a short while to come were like the Vietcong in later years: rather more so, because they possessed no rich supply line right into China.

Probably they were more like the Swiss, who, at approximately this same period, were similarly defeating armored knights with naked hands and a suddenly emerging national spirit.

It was at the time an extraordinary development, much more so than it would be today when all men take it for granted that they cannot be bullied from the top—at least not for long and with impunity. Today the people dictate, but in the thirteenth and fourteenth centuries there was a completely rigid social structure, especially where the feudal barons of Norman origin were in control. For the ordinary people suddenly to get together and dare to cock a snook at the castles was like a revolution of dogs and cats today. It was, for many of the armored knights, quite incredible. And some of them never got over the shock.

Edward I of England, "Hammer of the Scots," probably could not understand it at all. He had built strongholds all over the land and garrisoned them with well trained, heavily armed English fighters of the best type. He had imposed a rigid social system and laws and had already brought many new kinds of prosperity to an essentially primitive people. Relatives of his in the cassocks and mitres of the one and only Church had distributed thousands of pounds worth of charity and had patiently preached the Christian doctrine of turning the other cheek and of goodwill to all men. "*Why* do they hate me so much?" the unfortunate Edward must have secretly cried.

Wallace himself rapidly proved to be just one more typical, overreaching Scot. He should have been content with arousing the peasants continually to harry the hated English. No. Like all of his northern breed he must start marching south, into England, in order to steal cattle and women from those fat border counties of Northumberland and Cumberland.

Also he allowed little victories to go so much to his young head that he must proclaim himself Governor of Scotland and have the temerity to meet the English in open battle a second, fatal time.

Stirling was an English defeat thanks to the incompetence of de Warenne. Falkirk, not so far away both in place and time (1298) was a resounding triumph for English superiority in both courage and battle tactics. Wallace had carefully trained his "schiltrons" to stand stolidly with spears outpointed when the armored knights charged at them. But the English brought up their incomparable archers, whose longbows projected a hail of lethal arrows at the stolid ranks of spearsmen. Then, when the arrows had killed enough the mighty knights on their heavy carthorses would charge.

At Falkirk the Scots deserved to be defeated because they had come into the open with the wrong tactics and weapons. Wallace thereafter was a fugitive of the hills rather than a guerrilla leader, and seven years later he was captured by the English and put down like the dog he had (to them) been.

But he went into legend and poesy and song and marble. His statues still loom down and the memory of that impetuous young man's brief career still inspires Scotsmen to deeds of arms and to arguments in southern bars. "Scots wha hae wi' Wallace bled!"

It is extraordinary what a single brave man can achieve, especially if he is cut off at the height of his career before time can unmask him. Young Wallace's real achievement was twofold: (1) The stimulation of the Scots successfully to resist the English for a long time. (2) Robert the Bruce.

Robert was the grandson of the Norman baron whom Edward had considered as a possible candidate, with Balliol, for the old Scottish throne. His background was completely different from Wallace's. He was a Norman aristocrat, and although his family had acquired certain Scottish sentimentalities and roots in a short time, he was by no means the wild Caledonian patriot that later romantic liars made him out to be. Both he and his father were what the English later called "trimmers," which means they knew how to change sides and keep in power. The entire English story is really a history of successful "trimmers," right down to Winston Churchill.

Bruce possessed the inestimable advantage of a fierce temper allied to a shrewd political sense. The temper gave him irresistible courage in battle, and the political sense taught him suddenly, in 1305 when Wallace was executed, that Edward I of England was inexplicably faltering and maybe he could himself (with some vague claims of lineage) become a king.

He could not lose much in any case because he was at this time a hunted outlaw, having rather cholerically cut the throat, in a church of all places, of the Red Comyn, a similar Norman contender of the time.

Bruce collected together the scattered remnants of Wallace's patriotic and Corsican-type bands and not only used them properly as guerrillas but also applied the Norman know-how to their military training. And, in 1306, had himself proclaimed King of Scotland. He was very lucky, because next year Edward I died.

If Edward had lived a few years longer the history of Scotland and England would have been quite different. Edward might have been a Hammer but he was an extraordinarily good king and great statesman. Our modern parliamentary democracy, for all its faults, owes a great deal to him. He established the first Model Parliament in 1295. Also he settled the Welsh problem more or less permanently.

Edward II was the son of a too-strong father. He inherited strength but only in the form of cruelty, and believed in having a good time, and curried favor with favorites (who eventually deposed and murdered him in Berkeley Castle).

King Robert the Bruce probably had that adventure with the spider. He was not a real Scot by any means, but his policy of never giving up appealed greatly to a poor people in a hard land. It was essentially a Norman or Scandinavian policy—even a German policy—but it became a sentimental myth to the essentially unstable Scots.

Bruce continually harried the English in their Scottish castles, which fell one by one. When the English forces were too strong he invented a scorched earth policy to dismay them, and often the soldiery starved as a result. Edward II gave leading jobs to the wrong men and did not himself come to see what was wrong. The showdown was at wonderful Bannockburn on June 24, 1314. The flower of English chivalry came right down to earth for the first time ever. It was a complete, large scale defeat of the English knights and archers, who were driven back by the disciplined forces of Bruce into utter confusion. The English ran and were slaughtered amid the ruddy bogs and streams of what is still a sad, sad landscape.

In 1328, the year before he died, Robert the Bruce obtained from the Treaty of Northampton with England his final desire. The English thereby recognized the independence of Scotland and himself as permanent king (permanent until that death a year later).

It was in many ways a classic victory of Pyrrhus. The English had not easily relinquished their grip on the scorched earth of the north. Bruce's reign had been largely a series of forced marches among burning villages, and of conflicts between clans who quarrelled in peace and quarrelled in war. Agriculture and industry did not have a chance. The people often starved and never had a say in their own affairs. Bruce had to be a despot, and he was one. It was now, indeed, that the so-called government of the country had to turn originally to England's other enemy, France, for alliance and for aid. But the alliance was like that of a peasant with a harlot and the aid was given only at a price.

Robert was succeeded by his son King David II of Scotland, who reigned from 1330 to 1370, a long time for those days, but who made the usual Scottish mistake, in 1346, of taking an army down into England. There, near dire Durham, at Neville's Cross, while the best of the English were beating the French at Crecy, the ordinary yeomanry of the shires so roundly defeated the stupid invaders that King David himself was taken prisoner by a woman, Queen Philippa, who was looking after the realm while her husband Edward III was fighting the French. David was lucky to get back to Scotland in due course. There was still chivalry in the air those days, and family relationships meant something, especially between kingdoms.

For some 200 years thereafter Scotland had no worthwhile history, only the constant realization that she had missed the bus politically and could not really get along without England. She did her best, but became poorer and poorer. The Bruce dynasty came to an end with David and was succeeded by the less adventurous and distinguished Stuarts, a family that possessed very little sense of enterprise, not even in nomenclature. There were Robert II and Robert III and after that no fewer than five Jameses in a row, till Mary Queen of Scots led to a final James VI. Just one of them made a desperate bid to retrieve the ever-foundering fortunes of his land.

That was James IV, (1473–1513). Although he had been clever enough to marry Margaret, daughter of the great Tudor King of England Henry VII, he was the usual foolish Scot and invaded the south in 1513. At Flodden, near Coldstream in Northumberland, on September 9, the Scots suffered their greatest martial defeat by the English. The most remarkable of English climbers from the ranks arranged this, Cardinal Wolsey, and the Earl of Surrey made a good lieutenant on the field. James IV and nearly all his nobles and clan leaders were hopelessly slain.

Such a family as the Stuarts never really were outside the later plays of Eugene O'Neill. James I was captured by the English on his way to France in 1406 and held prisoner till 1424. He married Lady Jane Beaufort while still technically a prisoner and wrote a poem of love called *The Kingis Quair.* Eventually he was murdered by his best friends, who had doubtless had that poem read aloud to them once too often.

James II's reign, according to the books, was "troubled," but it lasted only a few years, at the end of which he was accidentally killed while besieging Roxburgh Castle and trying to deal with one of his naughty noblemen.

James III proved to be no more popular than his unfortunate father. He certainly reigned from 1469 till 1488, but at the age of 37 was murdered during a rebellion.

What hope could there ever be for a country that so constantly slaughtered its elected kings? How could Scots ever mock at the revolutions in Latin American republics or the occasional assassinations of presidents in the United States of America when their own history as an independent country is almost entirely a record of mayhem in high places?

James V succeeded his father who was cut down at Flodden. He swiftly went in for the royal sport of English-baiting. The English hit back at Solway Moss, 1542, another rousing defeat for Scotland, and the humbled king died soon after. His heir was an infant daughter, Mary.

Mary Queen of Scots has been written about so much that she has become a world legend, like William Tell or Napoleon Bonaparte.

Like them, however, she has almost completely disappeared as a person in the mingled flood of praise and blame. Either she's a high, romantic figure or a filthy scarlet woman. Of course she was neither, just an extremely attractive girl who had a great passion for men: and, bubbling with the blood of those essentially unlucky Stuarts she was bound to go wrong whatever she did. Rarely was there such a maladroit player at the card table of life. Consider the bare facts.

She was born in 1542, the year of her father's death. Henry VIII was beginning to grow monstrous on the English throne, and in 1543 concluded a shrewd treaty with Scotland, providing for perpetual peace between the two countries and, as a permanent earnest of this, the marriage eventually between his baby son Edward and the infantile Mary.

What did the Scots do? They deliberately sent the little girl in her swaddling-clothes to France.

There was, however, a very good reason for this. Thanks to intermarriages of the Stuarts with the English royal family it had come to pass that if the issue of Henry VIII for any reason failed then baby Mary would actually become heir to the English throne. That made her quite likely to be one more Stuart murdered if she remained in the British Isles. Was Scotland to be handed over to the hated English on a plate just because the heir to its throne was to be married eventually to the heir to the English throne of which she could also be the heir?

How much more clever to send her to France where yet another child was the king's son there, the Dauphin! The French might see that if their heir-apparent was eventually married to little Mary then there was a good chance of the English throne's becoming one more French possession.

The French did see this; and Mary was affianced to the Dauphin as soon as they could get the necessary papers drawn up. It was an extraordinarily fine stroke of policy and must have given Bluff King Hal in Windsor the Tudor equivalent of a heart attack.

Because bluff King Hal knew that there was something desperately wrong with his own issue. Probably as a result of the venereal disease from which the pleasure lover suffered, his children from those many wives were none of them very much good genetically. The boy Edward was a nice lad but hopelessly consumptive. The main daughter Elizabeth just would not look at the boys. She was brilliant at school but a sexual write-off. The other daughter Mary was a religious maniac with a strong vein of natural cruelty. She got her love life from countersigning orders for the public burning of Protestant martyrs, and of course she eventually married Philip of Spain. Henry knew the children were like this years before. In fact the whole of Europe knew it.

So poor little Mary, Mary all contrary (she was actually the original of the nursery rhyme) was from infancy the most important pawn in the political game of her time. At last Scotland had a weapon that it could use. The ridiculous Stuarts had by a miracle produced a potential winner at last.

It was all nominally done in the name of religion. Henry VIII to divorce one of his wives had broken with the Church of Rome and set up his own establishment, cashing in at the same time on the universal desire for ecclestiastical reformation. Scotland divided half and half between the old Catholic and the new Protestant faiths, but the ruling party that controlled the throne was largely traditionalist and therefore Catholic. And there was only a baby on the throne, being brought up in popish France to marry a Catholic king who might, with her, eventually be able to restore the old faith in England.

The child grew apace and prettily. We really know little about her as an actual person: only her deeds are left. But she must have possessed that surprisingly rare quality in womanhood (a quality her cousin Elizabeth of England most definitely did not possess) of being able to give pleasure to men and of *wanting to give it*. She could have become a film star, and if she had lived today other more educated women would naturally have called her a nymphomaniac. And, like all who are favored by the gods with a natural gift of inestimable value, she had to pay for it with rather more than the normal Stuart share of sheer bad luck.

They married her to that typically sickly French Dauphin in her teens and he very shortly became a king, Francis II, but died when she was only 19.

The most successful Scottish historian of modern times was George Macaulay Trevelyan, a descendant of the Macaulay who re-wrote history in the Whig interest more than a century before. And Trevelyan once described Mary on her arrival back in Scotland as only an "able, energetic and attractive widow." That neatly summarizes the way a certain party in the land has always regarded her. A widow at 19! She was not a widow but a comparatively untouched girl. And so unlucky.

Henry VIII had done his best to force the Reformation on Scotland as a matter of policy. He had repeatedly sent troops and ships north to break any Catholic resistance. Then he died, and the Protector Somerset continued the game. Its culmination was one more Scottish battle disaster, at Pinkie in 1547. Thereafter the old families of Catholics did not have a chance, even though the French did their best to help them (and help themselves to the Scottish spoils at the same time).

When the attractive young Mary arrived back in 1561 she found that the country under the English-imposed new Protestants was really against her. The common folk shouted at her "French whore" as soon as she arrived.

What had happened was that the more vigorous families of Lowland squires and the more subtle of the Highland nobles had summed up a kind of profit and loss account. Complete Scottish independence from England was not only impossible; it had resulted in grave wounds to the country, principally in trade. Catholicism was the natural religion of the old romanticism, but meant France and Spain and Italy as against England. So those families and nobles had gradually massed behind the agitators from England like John Knox who had been sent to back up the irresistible military presence. The true Parliament of the unfortunate country had gradually become the "Congregation of the Lord" or church assembly of the Covenanters. Marching all over the place in the name of religion, as Mahomet had done once he had grown out of his youthful spirituality, these people swiftly dominated the land.

So Mary, having lost her French kingdom thanks to the untimely death of her young husband, came back to Scotland to find that she was an old-fashioned Catholic from hated France and was not wanted there either. No wonder her father had died so soon after the Solway disaster, hearing of the birth of a daughter, and crying out at the age of 30: "The devil take it!"

Mary's court that she brought from France was gaudy with pleasure-loving, cultured young men and women. Today they would make some nice companionable society on a Greek or Bahaman riviera. They were no worse morally than the Covenanters who killed in the name of religion and who enjoyed clandestine rather than open sex. But it can be imagined how they appeared to the more simple folk of Scotland in those troubled days. Especially when it became known that Mary's party was all for the placing of her eventually on the throne of England that was so firmly occupied now by the formidable Elizabeth. The simple folk of Scotland had by now experienced enough of trying to do without England economically. They had been beaten right down to the ground.

And pretty young Mary continued to receive and to play all the wrong cards. She had to marry again, for the succession. Whom did

she choose? She chose her first cousin—which caused dark talk at once
on the banks and braes—and he was a particularly degenerate but frequently amusing member of the doomed house of Stuart called Henry,
Lord Darnley (born in England as the son of the Earl of Lennox, an
Englishman, the Stuart connection coming from his Douglas mother's
side).

Among her household was a secretary of Italian origin called David
Rizzio—again the fatal choice—and Mary listened to his shrewd,
Machiavellian advice about how she should keep her husband in his
place, and, specifically, not accord him the crown matrimonial. It has
of course been said that Rizzio was one more of her lovers, but that
is unestablished and in any case unimportant. What is important is
that Mary listened to the man and alienated the hot-headed Darnley
with his Douglas blood. Darnley assembled some swashbuckling
friends and entered the Edinburgh palace of Holyroodhouse one
evening when Mary was supping in a very small, panelled room with
Rizzio and some other courtier friends. They had the grace to knock
at the door but walked in with weapons drawn and made straight
for the secretary who instantly became Italian and crouched down by
the young Queen, clutching at her skirts. He was dragged away to
another room screaming and he was slain.

Not long ago it was still the custom to be shown the "stain" on the
floor of Rizzio's blood, that, it was claimed, could never be eradicated.
But the true stain was on the conscience of a Scotland that could
never cease to feel horror at what had once been its true fury.

The medical psychologists say that the infliction of pain arouses
sexual desire. Certainly Mary Queen of Scots went to bed with her
husband a few days after the murder of Rizzio and conceived a child
from the experience, who became James VI of Scotland and James I
of England and can be counted by the present Queen Elizabeth II
of England as a remote ancestor.

But it did not last. Darnley was not really a nice man, and Mary
was still a high-spirited girl. She became susceptible, to use no stronger
a word, to one of the Hepburns, the fourth attractive and very masculine Earl of Bothwell. She was able to claim, when she got a divorce
from him in 1570, that he had ravished her before marriage. The poor
girl. She was just too easy and always picked the wrong men.

Darnley had thrown his political weight about too much as the
newly-reconciled husband of the precarious Queen. All parties agreed
that he was a bad influence on her and could only lead the throne
to disaster. The strong Earl of Bothwell, as the Queen's latest lover,
got all parties together and arranged one more fatal plot. Darnley,

having fallen ill from the usual dissipation, was lying abed, in a lonely house at Kirk o'Field, Edinburgh. On February 10, 1567, the house was blown up with gunpowder, barreled nicely in the cellar. And afterwards Darnley's body was found in the garden. Had it been projected there by the explosion? Anyway, he had been strangled to death.

There was an enormous trial in Edinburgh a few weeks later, and the nation never ceased to talk of the implications. Had young Mary been involved? Maybe she had not, but to the simple Scottish folk she most certainly had. Strings were pulled for Bothwell and he was acquitted and rushed to the Queen. She must marry him. She refused. He actually abducted her. And, on May 15 that year, having divorced his wife (yes, of course he was married) he quite forcibly married his Queen.

Almost instantly the Scots arose everywhere and aimed to capture the Woman of Babylon and give her her deserts. In this they were enthusiastically aided by the English. Elizabeth of England sent supplies, men and instructions. But Bothwell was still irresistible and assembled an army, a little army of his friends. There was a battle, at Carberry Hill, and the Bothwell men were soundly defeated. Mary abdicated, and was taken on Elizabeth's orders to that island in Loch Leven which has been mentioned in a previous chapter of this book. That she had something which not all women possess is shown by the way she was able to persuade a young man of the house to help her escape, which she did in slim boy's clothes. She raised another army and was finally defeated at Langside, after which she made the greatest of all her many mistakes. She fled to England of all places, right into her vicious cousin's arms. Elizabeth received her graciously, like a cat. She put her in prison and kept her there until the end.

It is frequently said that Elizabeth showed her usual good sense and statesmanship in not destroying the lush Mary at once. She did not want to alienate the Scots, nor to show how easily a Queen like herself could be made mortal. This was probably not so. Elizabeth, most feline of monarchs ever, preferred to play the cat and mouse game. She kept little Mary wondering for 19 long years in various castles of the sleepy shires. She watched with interest while the stupid woman took part in Catholic conspiracies against the English throne. She did not execute Mary until the child was 45 years of age, and then only because her participation in the Babington plot was just a little too obvious. (Time and time again Mary had fallen for conspirators. She was one of the most consummate fall guys in all history.)

Fotheringay of the lovely name, in Northamptonshire, England, has a castle which is almost as romantic looking as its name. It is the suitable place where Mary Queen of Scots was beheaded.

The brisk Bothwell?

He fled to Norway after his last, fatal battle, and thence to Sweden. He also tried continually to conspire and was finally constrained by those who knew him best to stay put in a castle of Zeeland, where in 1578 he died, insane.

But history gave pretty Mary her revenge. Ripeness is all. Elizabeth of England, for all her character and statesmanship, was no good in bed. She died childless. Her heir on the throne of England had to be James VI of Scotland, the lineal descendant of her grandfather Henry VII, the child of Mary Queen of Scots and Darnley.

James himself had two children, Charles I, and a girl, Elizabeth. Charles was beheaded by Cromwell, and the girl suffered an even worse fate. She was married off to a fat and stuffy German princeling called Frederick, Elector of Palatine.

The decapitated Charles, King of England, left a son who became King Charles II, the Merrie Monarch, another son James who abdicated and left not only Queen Anne behind him but also James the original Jacobite, and a daughter Mary who married William of Orange the Hollander, whose son William III married his cousin the daughter of James II and, with her, occupied the English throne before cousin Anne (who was such a typically unfortunate Stuart: she had no fewer than 17 children of whom only one survived and he died at the age of 12).

William and Mary being similarly fruitless, the English crown eventually fell rather strangely upon the round head of George I, Elector of Hanover in Germany, owing to the fact that his grandmother had been James I's daughter Elizabeth. George I was the direct ancestor of the present British Queen Elizabeth II (although Scots still prefer that she be called Elizabeth I, there being no Great Britain when the first Elizabeth was on the English throne).

Prince Philip, Duke of Edinburgh, consort of Britain's present Queen, is a lineal descendant of the Stuarts also. His great-great-grandmother was Queen Victoria.

So Mary, Mary all contrary did not do so badly after all. They mocked at her and they cut her down, but her seed inherited the earth.

It is the custom to date the birth of Great Britain as a united kingdom from 1707, when an Act of Union was formally signed between England and Scotland and their Parliaments merged in one. But

Scotland really lost her independence and became virtually an English possession in 1603, more than a hundred years before, when Mary's son James inherited the English crown on the death of the great Queen Elizabeth.

It could have been the other way round. Scotland could have given England not only a king but also a government. There have been many historic cases where smaller countries have taken control of larger neighbors. But this was not to be.

Scotland had those continuous religious troubles on the one side, and, on the other, had been convinced by several centuries of hopeless struggles against the inevitable that England was the stronger country. It was as if she knew in her bones by now that she was destined to be an economic dependency of England and would make money out of it anyway.

James, described by Henry IV of France as "the wisest fool in Christendom," turned out to be the very worst monarch for a Scotland in tribulation. He was a modern intellectual before his time, brilliant, well-read, well-meaning, and quite without that common-sense which comes from experience of real as opposed to book life. He had, moreover, inherited his mother's and father's sense of sexual freedom, and, although productive enough of children, soon earned the reputation, among the dour Scots especially, of a typically foreign Sodomite. His friends were free-thinking and free-living, and he even flirted with *Spain*.

Knox's Calvinism had finally prevailed in Scotland, and James was in many ways quite a modern-thinking Calvinist himself. But what did he do? He came to the conclusion that the English type of Reformation and Church with Bishops was best, and sought immediately to impose this system upon the triumphant Scottish Presbyterians. This tactless behavior led eventually to open rebellion again in Scotland and helped Cromwell when he had to fight James's son Charles.

So, far from taking over England when a Scotsman became its king at last, Scotland continued to war with the south. Stuart was a six-letter word, but, among the ordinary people of the north, had increasingly a dubious four letters. This in 1638 flared into the final revolt of the Covenanters. Brother slaughtered brother and families extinguished themselves over minor points of ecclesiastical doctrine. It was very like the situation in Northern Ireland at this modern time of writing. It was quite irrational but revealed the culmination of a sickness in the land that had been festering ever since it had been implanted by the clever English.

The eventual antibiotic was administered by that shrewd, hard

Englishman Oliver Cromwell. The Scots had actually started his rebellion for him. Charles I was beheaded by Cromwell but destroyed
as a king by the fierceness of the revolt staged by the Scottish Covenanters. The great Montrose rallied the royalist clans fatally against
the Scottish Church and was inevitably defeated. Cromwell went north
and rewarded his helpers there with the most stern and efficient
system of government they had enjoyed for several hundred years.
It was sometime before the actual Act of Union but it was the real
act of union.

Cromwell forcibly united England and Scotland in a single Commonwealth, and it was done with the agreement of a majority of the
people in each country (otherwise, probably, it could never have been
done). Specifically in Scotland he allowed the sword-girt Presbyterian
Church to remain very much in being, but he forbade it to persecute
those who did not agree with it, and he told it bluntly that it could
not rule as a secular power within the State. Instead he allowed Scottish representatives to sit in the English Parliament for the first time,
and nicely corrupted the old school with a new system of free trade
which swiftly brought good money north. After which he took a lot
of the money back in the form of taxes to pay for stern garrisons
of English soldiers everywhere.

Thus upon the Restoration of Charles II in 1660 there were many
Scots who wished for real independence again and who actually tried
to obtain it. But it was too late. Oliver had administered the antibiotic and the country was really at rest, anxious only for more and
more of that wonderful English trade.

There were some 50 years of mingled disillusion and increasing
hope. The Stuarts were as crazy as usual. The restored Charles II
was stupid enough to deny Scotland the free trade that Cromwell had
given her. James II was no better. The Presbyterians were continually
given the excuse to think themselves persecuted by what they regarded as English lovers of hated Rome. In 1688 the British Isles
suffered another revolution, and once again it began in a Scotland that
considered itself wronged. But the real fire had died out and this
final uprising against a Catholic-seeming King was comparatively
tame. James just scuttled his ship and William and Mary came over
to countries that were eagerly awaiting them (not Ireland, but that
is another story). The Scots, as represented in Edinburgh by a very
religious Parliament, bargained usefully with the English. Might they
be granted virtual independence but also free trading rights if they
agreed to the accession of William and Mary to the joint throne?

Yes, they might; and under the new monarchy there was at least a measure of religious peace in the long-troubled northern land. There was, of course, an inevitable effort by the wild Highlanders, under Claverhouse, to drive the English soldiery back out of Scotland. This was crushed at the battle of Killiecrankie in 1689, where Claverhouse fell. And there was the foolish English mistake of Glencoe. But even that was a useful thing in that it demonstrated to the mass of the people that there was not really a hope against England.

In the final years before the Act of Union in 1707 it became quite obvious to all clear-thinking Scots that the country was just not viable in her present state, alone. She could have a Parliament in Edinburgh, and some measure of feudal pride in the glens, but agricultural methods were primitive, farm houses were hovels, the finest castles and mansions had neither windows nor carpets, and the children ran about on bare feet. Everyone knew the Bible by heart but there was such poverty in Scotland as had never been. Whereas over the border, down in England, the land was smiling and even the peasantry was by comparison rich. London was becoming one of the most affluent metropolises of the world, already sucking in wealth from overseas colonies and trading enterprises without compare.

At the same time English statesmen were worried about the succession again, noting that their extraordinary Queen Anne, who had succeeded William and Mary, was unable to produce a living heir in spite of all her prodigious efforts. They had already turned to Hanover and knew that those stolid Germans would cause far less trouble on the throne eventually than one of the Frenchified and decadent Jacobites (see previous involved genealogy). But that Jacobite party had adherents in Scotland, representing the worst of the Stuarts.

The English politicians told Scotland that they could have a complete economic union with England on condition that the Hanoverian succession was agreed and that the Scottish Parliament and Privy Council should be permanently merged in that of England.

Scotland agreed and was at once made and lost. She was made economically, and during the next two hundred years waxed fat and prosperous on the English connection. Her people were stimulated as never before to work hard and to invent and to write. Under the Union she gave the world much of those industrial and intellectual gifts that ignorant foreigners always thought were English in origin.

But as a nation she was lost. The Jacobite rebellions of 1715 and 1745 were romantic but hopeless last kicks of an already dead donkey. And after that there was absolutely no more Scottish history as such.

11

PEOPLE

NATIONS are judged not by the height of their mountains nor their hours of sunshine nor even by the size of their cities, but by the achievements of their people. These may be in religion, the arts, the sciences, philosophy, war, even in the industrial crafts. How does Scotland rate?

A patriot of this country has plenty to say. It is not a modest country. Your true Scot boasts in a flagrant manner that not even a first-generation Californian could hope to emulate, and he leaves most Texans standing. More fights have broken out in bars all over the world because Scotsmen have been insulted than for any other cause. The most ignorant Scot will deliberately tell stronger men that his country has produced the best poets and raspberries and ships and statesmen and pop singers as if he really wants to fight.

This would have earned the Scots a terrible reputation if they had not been so nice with it. Because they are nice, among the nicest in the world (there, a typical Scot begins to boast again).

They are nice as human beings, generous, helpful, warm-hearted, and completely lacking that artificial, inhibited manner which makes Englishmen, by comparison, not so nice.

They make excellent colonists because they do not insist upon doing in Rome what Rome does not do. Chameleon-like, they adapt themselves to each new environment and become popular there for that among other reasons.

Even their accent makes them liked. It is somehow childish and homely. It is the accent not of the great lord who knows he is the appointed master of the world, but of the funny old retainer who does the dirty work and is loved because he is so amusing.

And when the inevitable Scottish boasting begins it is quite impressive in its way. Let us regard the substance of it, as it would be uncouthly mouthed at the beginning of one of those alcoholic quarrels in bars.

"Where is your Jesus Christ, your Buddha, your Mahomet, even your Moses?" the teaser asks; and the plucky little Scot shouts in reply: "Och, have you not heard of John Knox? Have you forgotten where David Livingstone came from, and Mary Baker Eddy? Are those not achievements for you, unless you want to go back to Columba and Ninian and Margaret and the rest of those who brought real Christianity to the British islands?"

And it would be a brave man indeed who would interrupt the flow of eloquence by pointing out that Margaret was an Englishwoman, and Ninian a paid servant of Rome, and Columba a descendant of Irish kings, and Mary Baker Eddy a real American if ever there was one no matter the degree of Scottish blood in her, and David Livingstone primarily an explorer who worked for the English.

As for John Knox, no one would have the temerity to tell a Scot the real facts to his face.

Nor inform the hot-headed patriot that far from giving the world anything important in the way of religion—anything like Egypt or Persia or India or China or Israel or Italy or Germany or even England gave—his poor Scotland merely set an example to others of the worst kind of un-Christian behavior within her too-numerous churches. Next time a history of intolerance is written the fattest chapters should be devoted to Scotland, even fatter than those dealing with Spain.

Scotland could have used her Christian enlightenment to spread a doctrine of sweetness and light throughout the world. Knox could have been a better Mahomet or Gautama Buddha, or at least a Confucious with a Doric accent. Instead of that the little country just set an example of quarrelling and persecution, and Knox, with all his big ideas, was a thoroughly bad man.

What about poetry?

Scotland produced in Robert Burns a man who wrote some fine lyrics for songs. In our time, with the right kind of promotion, he might have had several hits on Broadway at once. But as a writer of English he was wonderful only that he was able to write at all. In the eighteenth century his appearance and success was like an Australian aborigine getting into best-selling hard covers today. His greatest achievement (poets being the unacknowledged legislators of the world) was to put over the idea at a time of incipient revolution everywhere that "a man's a man for a' that."

Burns was a good and interesting minor poet in the Scottish vernacular, but a little jumping flea beside the towering giants of the ancient world such as Homer and Virgil and Horace and Sappho, and beside the true, king-size poets of our modern civilization such as Shakespeare and Spencer and Milton and Keats and Coleridge and Tennyson, not to mention quite a few Germans, French, Italians, Spaniards, Russians and Americans.

Maybe Walter Scott set an example of literary industry to the world that has helped to inspire as well as educate others, and he was a supremely able public relations man for his sad, small country. In many ways he created the Scotland that most people know. He made of little scuffles and a few half-savage customs the stuff of a great tapestry whereon battles take place between giants and kings and gods, and tartans and pibrochs and claymores become heroic instruments of death.

But Walter Scott never spoke his mind right out and contributed nothing to world thought. Neither his English prose nor his interpretation of history came near to the achievement of such a comparatively unknown one-book Englishman as the Winwood Reade who wrote *The Martyrdom of Man*. All that Scott achieved was success; and his work will not have any lasting influence on the progress of humanity.

With all this Burns and Scott were writers who represented their country well and have given infinite pleasure to many, especially Scottish readers. But Burns was not comparable with a Shakespeare or even a Keats as a writer, a poet and a thinker, and neither can Scott be compared with a Balzac or a Tolstoy or even with a Thomas Hardy as a novelist capable at once of writing fine prose and revealing the true depths of human character.

Scotland produced many other successful writers, such as Robert Louis Stevenson and James Barrie. Both of those wrote better English than Burns or Scott. But they were in no sense world figures. Maybe if Scotland was blasted to ashes by atomic warfare it might be remembered for at least the wrong-headed freak of Burns and the immense industry of Scott, but would anyone really point at the ruins and say "That gave us R.L.S., or Barrie, or James Bridie or Eric Linklater, or S. R. Crockett or John Buchan or George Douglas Brown?" James Thompson, author of *The City of Dreadful Night*, was a typical Scot but only a minor writer. And Smollett was not really important save that he came from near Glasgow.

No, the literary achievement of Scotland is more positive than her religious contribution, but not more so than that of a Portugal with Camoens and de Moraes, and a nineteenth century America with Emerson, Thoreau, Holmes, Longfellow, Hawthorne, Whitman, Melville, Poe and Bierce. Indeed that early American harvest although never in the highest class, might arguably be regarded as far greater than all Scotland's in two thousand historic years.

And in the other arts there is, alas, scarcely anything that can be said unless the crafts of the Adam family be included under the heading. Robert Adam did not create but he codified an important architectural style, that of the classical revival. He planned the building of habitable houses with his own idea of what were Graeco-Roman embellishments, and similarly he designed furniture and other appurtenances to everyday living that are remembered and copied. He was, however, essentially a technician and not an artist, as have been all the Scots who usefully contributed to our civilization.

In the graphic arts Scotland gave us only Raeburn and Ramsay, who were competent portrait painters but did not draw a single line which helped to change the world or their art; and there has been no Scottish composer of international standard. A Jew, Mendelssohn, had to be invited to Scotland to give it the only half-great musical expression of its essential spirit which it has ever had; and the true artistic sound of the country is the savage skirl of the bagpipes and lamenting songs of the common people as rewritten for Victorian parlors by some rather remarkable spinsters. This is often more interesting than the comparable folk music of Ireland and the American West, but of course cannot be discussed in the same breath as Mozart, Bach and even a second-class Englishman like Edward Elgar.

In the sciences we come nearer home, although Scotland produced no one of great importance until she had been in existence for centuries and then had become completely merged into the English culture. John Napier invented logarithms in the seventeenth century. James Watt, described already as the inventor of the steam engine, was a typical precursor of several important names in the nineteenth century in that he mainly applied his science to what would have practical value and make money. Scotland has produced few great theoretical scientists, unless Ernest Rutherford, the New Zealander who worked on the foundations of atomic theory, be admitted to the pantheon because his family originally came from the north.

James Clerk Maxwell of Edinburgh (1831–79) was the greatest Scottish scientist as such. It can be demonstrated that if Scotland only produced him it had thereby changed part of history. Maxwell was the pioneer physicist who, in his short life, uncovered many of the secrets of matter which have enabled us to enlarge the control of our environment in our time, particplarly in gases, optics, color sensation, electricity and magnetism. It was his theoretical work in magnetism that made possible the development of telegraphy, the telephone and radio. But, being a typical Scot, he worked chiefly on what could have swift practical application.

That application was largely the work of another Edinburgh-born man, Alexander Graham Bell (1847–1922), who was educated at Edinburgh and London but went at the age of 23 to Canada and thence to Boston. There, not unsuitably, he opened a school for teachers of the deaf, and became professor of vocal physiology at the university. His brave Scottish efforts to help the hard of hearing, combined with his reading of Maxwell's works on electricity and magnetism, led to his epoch-making invention of the telephone in 1876.

Perhaps an even more typical Scottish scientific pioneer was the inventor of television, John Logie Baird. Unlike Bell he did not have the sense to emigrate to North America, but struggled against the dead hands of an already decadent England. He was born at Helensburgh in 1888 and worked in London commerce until the age of 34 when ill health cut short his money-making. He started to work on a televisor and a noctovisor, and four years later he demonstrated before the Royal Institution a transmission of human faces along waves from a distant transmitter to a screen. This created the kind of sensation that makes academic scientists scoff and industrial spies get to work. Baird nearly got it over as the basis of the first television broadcasting system, but the German Post Office acquired a formula and became the real pioneers in 1929. The British Broadcasting Corporation started to produce television programs soon after but eventually adopted a system developed by the Marconi-E.M.I. companies instead of Baird's.

In 1941, during the Second World War, this Scotsman came up with colored television, but he died five years later without much honor. His achievement and his failure were indeed typical of the strange northern people that had produced him.

Who *applied* those magnetic and sonorous inventions propertly for the first time to the services of society? It was one more Scotsman of the most rabid type, John Charles Walsham Reith, whose career reads like a potted history of the Scottish tragedy all over again.

Reith was born in 1889, son of the Very Rev. George Reith, of Aberdeen and Glasgow; and he was directly descended from those Covenanters who had marched about preaching of hell fire in intervals of unmercifully beating up anyone who disagreed with them. He looked like a Covenanter, or New Englander of the *Scarlet Letter* days, being six feet six inches tall, dark, his grim face scarred by a war wound, his mouth eternally set in a thin, down-turning line, and his fierce eyes deep under great thick brows.

He had the mind of a Puritan, and obviously disciplined himself mentally every day of his life, having the kind of spartan habits that cynics rather unfairly associate with their own kind of fantasy world.

He was a superb organiser, an office martinet of great self-confidence, but, being a Scot, succumbed only too frequently to the weakness of telling the truth not only about others but also about himself, the last being the unpardonable sin in England. "You are a fool," he would say, "and your idea just won't work." After which he would add: "I will rough out a scheme myself. I am very good at that sort of thing."

He began as an engineer. Every second Scotsman started thus in the iron age of Edwardian Britain. Then the First World War erupted and young Reith soon became a hero, a Major in the regiment of Royal Engineers who constantly set an example to everyone about him for courage. The enemy must have feared him, but his own men even more. That scar on his face was traced by the bullet of a sniper who had probably been drawing a bead on the giant for a long time. In old age Reith wrote a book about those experiences, *Wearing Spurs,* which is as well written and stirring as it is basically brash.

After that war young Reith marched back to the engineering firm of Beardmores in Coatbridge, Scotland, and soon became what they call general manager in those parts. He could never have been anything but a general manager. Scots like John Reith never filled subordinate positions.

Soon after that the British Government decided that the infant craft of radio broadcasting was potentially too dangerous a medium to be left in private hands. Sound broadcasting was made a State monopoly, and once again a post of general manager was advertised. John Reith read about it and marched up to London. He became the first general manager of the British Broadcasting Company, although he knew little about wireless telegraphy and popular art. There were only 56,000 licences at that time, 1922, and Reith was given a staff of three.

Just over 15 years later, when Reith finally resigned from his ultimate job of Director-General of the B.B.C. or British Broadcasting Corporation (he probably invented those magniloquent terms) the licences had increased to 8,700,000, and the staff of three to 4,000.

The man was as much a pioneer Socialist as Stalin, only probably more efficient and less cruel. He did not think of the beauty that broadcasting could create, nor even of the happiness it could disseminate. Like his Covenanter ancestors he considered only the moral and educational aspects of the new medium. The people must be given not what they wanted but what he, John Reith, considered would be *good* for them. Therefore broadcasting must be a State monopoly. It was the exact opposite of the American approach at that period. America then not only had a Statue of Liberty but believed in it. What Reith created in England was a strong discipline for the people, imposed from on top. It was one of the beginnings in England of the Welfare State.

But of course it had its good side. The B.B.C. as created by Reith supported the arts and remained aloof from everyday, City Hall politics. It eschewed box office and its concomitants, cheap pornography and sensationalism. It was just like Edinburgh, elegant, grey, respectable, bleak, comparatively blameless, wholly dignified and very, very successful.

Reith was the headmaster of a good school or the feared rector of a great college. He imposed a religious-type discipline that educated a whole new generation of half-dedicated young men. The B.B.C. manner became the most important and admired in international broadcasting. The best of the American chains carefully modeled itself on it, and outstanding U.S. broadcasters like Ed Murrow were essentially B.B.C. men, in their hearts if not in their actual upbringing.

Foreigners think of certain British institutions which were in their way spotless and above approach like some of the ancient orders of chivalry. They were the Royal Navy, the great public schools, the Battle of Britain R.A.F., and Reith's B.B.C.

But of course something went wrong. Maybe it was just too unnatural. Or too Scottish. Anyway, Reith worked harder than anyone in Britain for just over those 15 years and then fell. The full story of that palace revolution remains yet to be told. Official secrets in Britain are much more secret than those in America. Reith himself gave the official version in his autobiography *Into the Wind*. (He was so much the humorless Scot that he would never have seen anything funny in that title.) He implied that in 1938 the British Broadcasting Corporation was finally created and so smooth-running that there was no more for such an energetic man as the Master to do. He wrote complacently: "I thought with quiet satisfaction of the vast and flawless efficiency of the organization."

Then he tells us in that revealing book how his ambitions were limitless. Britain needed him for much more than broadcasting. He could be the better Napoleon of his time. He had all the qualifications save a few. He could apply to the country, indeed to the world as a whole, those same methods that had created the B.B.C., and, in an age of Hitlers and Stalins and Mussolinis, who could resist him?

It seems, therefore, that Reith left his real lifework partly in order to achieve greater ambitions. But he also left because he had to. He was growing just a little bit too big for his boots, and that in England is always the prelude to a resounding and lasting crash. As soon as people in England become too successful, or too aware of being too successful, they are automatically brought down. Consider all the great favorites of the public in the last hundred years. Each was cut down to size ultimately, from Lloyd George onwards and even including Winston Churchill and the Beatles. England had just one dictator, Oliver Cromwell, and never wanted another.

Reith rarely came to the microphone save on really important occasions. Thus he personally announced the death of King George V and the abdication of another failed favorite, Edward VIII (who had committed the ultimate crime of desiring to marry not just an American but also a divorcée).

Meanwhile the Director-General had engaged in enormous disputes with not only his Board of Governors but also those Postmasters-General of the Government who nominally had responsibility for broadcasting. And he had in particular turned his awe-inspiring frown on two irresistible aspects of contemporary life. One was the infant television and the other was the remarkable man who saved his country in the Second World War. He liked neither TV nor Winston Churchill.

Both represented what a Covenanting Scot must most oppose in society, the gay and the aristocratic principles. (Oliver Cromwell would have been wholeheartedly with him there.)

Television meant the vile theatre on the screen and leg shows and all the concomitants of an ineffable *Variety*. The human voice could be controlled, save for occasional innuendoes, but not the human body and its brash, cigar-sucking promoters.

Later in life Reith actually appeared on TV, being interviewed by Malcolm Muggeridge and he admitted significantly that while German bullets had not caused him the slightest concern in the First World War he was *afraid* of the television camera.

As for Churchill, he represented not only the English snobbery of the upper classes but also the broad-minded, turncoat world of the arts and literature. Reith would probably have said that Winston was not the sort of man you could trust. (He had dared once to refuse him broadcasting time.)

The unhappy giant walked out of Broadcasting House, Langham Place, leaving behind the plaque with the Latin inscription and his name. He became Chairman of Imperial Airways, which he swiftly transformed into what became known in an illiterate age as B.O.A.C. His job was to create another socialistic type of state corporation, and he did this job well in a very short time, but it was demotion and he knew it.

Two years later Britain was defenseless against Germany, and Churchill had received his call. Reith thought there might be an equal opportunity for him, so he entered politics and was elected to Parliament. He swiftly became Minister of Information, then Minister of Transport, and, in that same momentous year 1940, was created Lord Reith. But this kept him out of really active politics in the House of Commons and prevented him from ever becoming Prime Minister. Soon after he was transferred to the dim-sounding Ministry of Works. There he mouldered masterfully for a while before being made Director of the Admiralty's Combined Operations Material Department. That meant organizing supplies for part of the British end of D-day. It was important work, done almost perfectly, but the end of a dream.

The Scotsman bitterly realized this himself, writing to Churchill: "You could have used me in a way and to an extent you never realized. Instead of that there has been the sterility, humiliation and distress of all these years—'eyeless in Gaza'—without even the consolation Samson had in knowing it was his own fault."

There was the real, stupid man talking. The Biblical references were typical of his breed. And it *had* been his own fault, as Churchill swiftly told him in reply. The greater man had to point out that Reith could have had the important jobs but there had been "too much opposition." People had said that "you were difficult to work with."

Without friends in a tight little village like England you are lost, and Reith had alienated the right people not only by his dictatorial efficiency but also by his stern, Puritannical manners at the beginning of a new, permissive age. He couldn't smile and he couldn't let his hair down. He was that sort of Scot.

They continued to give him second-class jobs that paid good money. They are fundamentally a decent people. He organized what were known as Commonwealth Telecommunications, and created the new town of Hemel Hempstead, and the National Film Finance Corporation.

Afterwards there was a job at the Colonial Development Corporation. The Labor Government which Britain preferred to Churchill after the war had lost millions at this crackbrained scheme for revivifying Africa. Reith worked hard again and turned the loss into a profit. Scotsmen have their faults but they can do that sort of thing.

Afterwards he just fought against the introduction of commercial television—and came full circle when he achieved the highest ambition of many people in the north, becoming Lord High Commissioner to the General Assembly of the Church of Scotland.

He died in 1971. His married life had been impeccable and he left a son and heir and a daughter, also that lasting monument of the B.B.C.

The purest application of science is medicine. Few real happinesses have come to mankind from aircraft, radio or the atom bomb, and plastic kitchens with dishwashers are no more joyous than their wooden predecessors with iron ranges and stone sinks. But discoveries which lessen pain and prolong life are uplifting for some people, especially those who dislike funerals and get frightened when they come out in spots.

Maybe the Scots learnt in the late eighteenth and early nineteenth centuries how to become doctors because there was money in it down England way. Perhaps they just had to learn about medicine to avoid complete racial suicide from the filth which streamed from their middens and the lung diseases which were encouraged by their terrible climate. There is a possibility also that, a deeply religious people, they liked occasionally to help each other.

Anyway the Scots play as large a part in the modern history of medicine as any people and more than many. Perhaps their contribution can be compared only with those of the Jews, the Americans and the French. Medical schools at the nineteenth century universities of Edinburgh, Glasgow and St. Andrews became world famous and eventually attracted students from deep jungles and wide deserts. The typical family doctor in popular English novels at the period when fiction still sold was nearly always an ageing man with gruff manners and a Scottish accent.

And Scotland gave us at least four medical geniuses who achieved more than all the scientists put together of some much larger countries.

The first was John Hunter, who lived from 1728 until 1793. He came from Lanarkshire but naturally took advantage of the Act of Union to go to London to work, at the celebrated St. George's Hospital, where he became a surgeon. This was at a time when surgeons operated with rusty saws and stained knives on people who were held down and gagged lest they ran away or woke the neighbors.

Hunter was the first modern surgeon in that he operated not as a butcher but as a practical scientist. He studied anatomy carefully and codified his findings in academic form. He was the founder of pathological anatomy, which means examining dead bodies in order to find what once made them tick, and specifically he was the inventor of an early, quite successful method of ligating aneurysms, or tying up arteries that have become dangerously swollen. He created one of the few museums which does not lull the beholder into a state of excruciating boredom. This, known as the Hunterian Collection, is visited by all young doctors at the Royal College of Surgeons in London still, and the sight of those bottled pieces of former humanity helps to harden them.

John Hunter killed himself with a certain measure of poetic justice. He had the wrong idea that both of the venereal diseases might be the same and this was seemingly confirmed by a typical Scottish experiment. Hunter inoculated himself with a patient's pus and it so happened that the patient was suffering from both gonorrhea and syphilis. In the eighteenth century they did not do things by halves. Hunter caught both diseases, and, before he died, proclaimed erroneously that they were one and the same malady. He died from a syphilitic aortic aneurysm, being too sick to deal with it properly himself by his celebrated method.

Hunter's elder brother William was almost as famous at the time, but rather less important now, being a pioneer in obstetrics, a science which has since advanced far beyond him. His magnum opus, *The Anatomy of the Gravid Uterus*, chiefly has interest today because it was printed by John Baskerville, one of the finest English typographers; and its 34 copper plates are works of art as well as weird anatomical illustrations.

The first Hunter taught surgeons of the world how and where to cut. But was quite unable to stop his victims from shouting aloud. This supreme act of humanity we owe to James Young Simpson. He was another product of early nineteenth century Edinburgh, became a famous obstetric surgeon, then evidently could not stand the shrieks of pain, because he experimented with chloroform and successfully introduced it as one of the first viable anaesthetics, in 1847 when he was only 36 years of age.

It is possible that Simpson's breakthrough might be regarded as one of the most important in human history, but of course only by those who have actually writhed with agony themselves while giving birth to a difficult child. It is understandable that many medical men who had not themselves experienced such pain should condemn the use of chloroform as productive only of dangerous side effects. But it was a Scotsman, Simpson, who first taught us how to operate without pain. He got his reward for it, a baronetcy, which meant that he and his male heirs would perpetually be called "Sir."

But if the surgeon knew not only how to cut but also how to stop the screaming, he did not, alas, know how to keep it clean. Every second patient died not from his initial disease or a bungled operation, but from infection that leapt from breaths and from dirty hospital walls into the wounds. So a practical Scottish scientist with an eye on the main chance was needed again. He was Joseph Lister.

Lister was born in 1827 and became professor of surgery at Glasgow in 1860 after studying at Edinburgh. He was a good surgeon himself but found that too many of his patients died after the cut for no good reason. He got his clue from Pasteur's work on microorganisms and he introduced, against the loud-mouthed protestations of his colleagues and minions, not only scrubbings of wards and theatres with disinfectant fluids and sterilizing of instruments, hands and clothes, but also the placing of pieces of linen, carbolic-soaked, into operative wounds. He was proved triumphantly right at once. Patients ceased to die so much or to suffer from so much suppuration and gangrene after operations. He was rightly given a peerage, and became the first doctor ever to sit in the House of Lords.

Thanks to Hunter, Simpson and Lister, all of them practical, clever Scots, the human death rate was considerably reduced. That might perhaps be regarded as an achievement, although Malthus would not have agreed. But then Malthus, who revealed that nature worked chiefly with death as an instrument of progress, was an Englishman, born nicely at Guildford in Surrey.

There were so many lesser Scottish pioneers in medicine that to list them would require many pages. Typical of these was the Ronald Ross who worked with Manson to conquer malaria. He served in the Indian Medical Service and painstakingly tracked down the malaria germ to the stomach of the anopheles mosquito. He was only one of many Scotsmen who won a Nobel Prize.

It was significant that the most famous Scottish scientists were those who applied their science to everyday purposes, and that nothing remotely like an Einstein ever came from Edinburgh. This observation will be carried still further if the Scottish contribution to the industrial crafts be properly regarded.

James Watt invented the steam engine. Another man from the north took Watt's invention and applied it to the steam hammer. This was James Nasmyth of Edinburgh, whose other, typically nineteenth century achievements included various hydraulic apparatuses and a planing machine.

William Symington was born in that fecund county Lanarkshire in

1763. First he applied the Watt steam engine to a road locomotive. Then he put the engine in a boat, the first steamship, which he tried out, not too successfully, in 1787–8. The celebrated Robert Burns was present at one of the trials. A better ship, the *Charlotte Dundas,* was sailed very successfully in 1802, just five years before the American, Robert Fulton, launched that epoch-making *Clermont* (which is often regarded as the first even though Fulton got most of his ideas from Symington and Watt).

Meanwhile an ingenious people had been looking dubiously at the muddy cart-tracks which in the eighteenth and early nineteenth century were all the Industrial Revolution had for roads. One of them was born in Ayr, not far away from Burns again, John Loudon Mc-Adam, and he invented the process of roadmaking which later became universal, that of pulverizing stone into small pieces of uniform size and applying them to the bed of the road with heavy pressure and a watering can. It seems such a simple and unimportant idea that McAdam's subsequent immortalization in the word "macadam" might arouse wonder at the gullibility of human beings. But it did transform the roads of the whole world and is still a basic principle of highway construction. Prior to McAdam there had only been mud, right back to the time of the Romans, whose Empire was largely the product of roads made from solid blocks of stone as will be seen in Italian towns to this day.

The method of macadamizing was first tried out on a large scale by Thomas Telford, a Scottish shepherd's son who became a poet and then thought better of it, going to the other extreme as an engineer who opened up northern Scotland for the first time by constructing some 920 miles of new highway through the mountains. It was Telford who built the Caledonian Canal, as well as many aqueducts and bridges, including the lovely structure over the Menai Strait in Wales which was the first British application of the suspension principle.

About the same time William Murdock of Boswell's Auchinleck (Ayrshire again) was inventing the system of gas lighting which partly illuminated the murkier depths of the Victorian age.

And of course it was a Scotsman, roundly named Kirkpatrick Macmillan, who set to work in 1839 and invented the first piece of machinery which could remotely be called a bicycle. He was usefully a blacksmith's son, but did not get far on his clumsy development of a hobby-horse with treadles that became pedals. Nor did anyone else, until the Scotsman John Boyd Dunlop invented the pneumatic tire. Dunlop was born in Ayrshire. The county is still redolent of Dunlops, although most of them nowadays are engaged in breeding cows. The original, born in 1840, was a veterinary surgeon who went to Belfast, where his little daughter entered for a school race on a primitive tricycle. Brilliantly Scottish, the not-so-young father (he was then 47) bound the wheels of the tricycle with rubber hose and inflated them, tying the ends with string. Whether the little girl won the race is not certain, but Dunlop instantly knew that he had a fortune if he could develop it. He took out a patent for a pneumatic tire and went into partnership with another Scot, R. W. Thomson, and founded the Dunlop Rubber Company.

All the same bicycles and not even early automobiles were much good in the Scottish climate without a measure of leakproof sartorial protection: but fortunately Charles Macintosh (1766–1843) had already invented the mackintosh (spelt that way eventually because it was harder). He was a manufacturing chemist, who thought of lining fabric with a rubber solution. It might be described as a characteristically Scottish solution of the British weather problem.

Then there was the Glasgow professor William Thomson Kelvin, who, similarly faced with the meteorological problems of British mariners, invented an improved compass, an automatic sounding line, a tidal gauge, a stranded cable and various gadgets used in telegraphy, also the second law of thermodynamics. He deservedly did well out of it, ending as a baron and a name on a park.

Or Sir James Dewar (1842–1923). He was a pioneer chemist and physicist and gave us the vacuum flask, but possibly his greatest invention, from the viewpoint of an essentially warlike people, was the explosive known as cordite (no connection, of course, with Dewar's whisky). John Rennie, unsuitably born at a place called Phantassie, built several of London's famous bridges.

Values mean what people think are important; and a foremost Scottish value has always been martial distinction. The Scot has many kinds of inferiority complex, derived from the essential poverty of his small land and from his failure to resist the superior power of the English. But he believes in his heart that he provides the world's fiercest and cleverest fighting man, and perhaps he does—under the command of another people. In this he resembles the Italian, whose modern failure in Italian armies as such will contrast so strangely with his individual courage and cunning.

Throughout history the Scotsman, especially as employed in the service of foreigners, has gained a reputation for superb bravery and irresistible ferocity as a fighter. A vast number of decorations for valor have been won by him everywhere, especially those which have some monetary value.

It is a fact, however, that since Wallace and Bruce the country has produced no military commanders of surpassing genius, only the best kind of G.I.s under foreign command. Some history books describe Haig as the winner of the 1914–1918 war, but others condemn him as unimaginative and prodigal of men's lives. Certainly he possessed none of the obvious brilliance of comparable Irishmen in command. There is no Scottish saviour of Europe such as Arthur Wellesley, Duke of Wellington, or even the Montgomery and Alexander who won decisive victories in the Second World War.

On the other hand the Scots, like the Swiss, have provided a useful stiffening in foreign armies, and, with typical colonizing facility, have got themselves into some very odd places. Way back in the eighteenth century one Samuel Greig (1735–88) more or less founded the Russian Navy, and took it into the Eastern Mediterranean to defeat the Turks at Chesmé. It is interesting to think that he might have been related to the Aberdeenshire family which produced the composer Edvard Grieg after a member had emigrated to Norway.

And, believe it or not, a virtual founder of the American Navy, John Paul Jones, was also once a rear-admiral in the Russian Navy and served similarly against the Turks in the eighteenth century Mediterranean. This Scotsman with the Welsh name was born in Kircudbright, 1747, and went to sea as a trader and slaver. He was very tough. While a young master of an old wooden sailing ship in the West Indies he had to tackle a similarly brutal member of the crew who was killed. Back in Scotland, Jones was accused of murder, so returned to the Caribbean for evidence in support of his innocence. There his crew mutinied and he had to kill the ringleader and escape to the American colonies, where he had a Virginian brother. On the outbreak of war he got a privateer's licence from Congress and made a swift specialty of the English convoys. Four years later the French put him in charge of a naval expedition, which he led successfully against the English for two years. He returned to America in 1781 to perform more doughty deeds on behalf of the colonists; and his example and his organizing genius then were responsible for a tradition that became the American Navy. He tried finally to do the same in Russia but did not make the right kind of gestures towards Catherine the Great, and lost his job. Like so many other fallen Lucifers he went to France to die.

One of Frederick the Great's most efficient field marshals was James Keith from Aberdeen, whose eventual reward was to be made Governor of Neuchâtel, where he further distinguished himself by giving some brief sanctuary to Rousseau.

When Napoleon went to work at Wagram he had a similar Scottish assistant named the Duke of Taranto (born Macdonald) who, many experts say, was the real winner of the battle; and this man's artillery commander was the Comte Lauriston, another product of the north.

Napoleon reached Moscow but was nicely harried on his way back by a Scotsman in the service of the Russians named Prince Barclay de Tolly (from Aberdeenshire).

The Scots have similarly won a deserved reputation for financial acumen, but once again this quality did not display itself until a foreign country gave it a chance. The first of the great Scottish manipulators of money was that William Paterson who, in 1694, was permitted to organize not only the Bank of England but also the *National Debt*. Both institutions made possible the industrial and commercial expansion of the modern world. Paterson was in a sense the man who invented credit, and was thus responsible for the backside of the same animal, which is currency inflation.

Paterson's good work was carried a step forward by John Law of Edinburgh (1671–1729). He founded, in 1716, France's first bank, the *Banque Générale*. The following year he established the Louisiana Company, which, being given a virtual monopoly of trade in the southern American colonies, could have become wealthy beyond the screams of avarice. Alas, Law was just a financier, and was not backed up by the right men and guns. He extended the operations of the Company to Asia, and merged it with his bank in 1720, but, when the Scotsman went to Venice to die in 1729, everything collapsed. (And in 1803 Napoleon sold the entire "Louisiana" territory to the United States for a few million dollars, and what did they make out of it? Just Louisiana itself, and Arkansas, Missouri, Nebraska, Iowa, South Dakota, as well as parts of North Dakota, Minnesota, Kansas, Oklahoma, Colorado and Wyoming.)

With the examples of Paterson and Law behind them the Scots steadily emigrated as financiers during succeeding epochs of western development. Banks, insurance companies, investment trusts, stock market mergers in Britain, America, Canada, Australia, South Africa, New Zealand and many other places were established and staffed, at the tops. A typical joke of the early twentieth century was: Old mother to Scotsman on a visit home: "And how did ye get on with the English people, Jock?" Jock: "Och, I had no opportunity for getting to know them. I only met the heads of departments."

They did so well as managers and manipulators of money because centuries of poverty had taught them how to keep expenses down and put something aside for a rainy day. The methods employed were extreme carefulness in bookkeeping and expenditure, and a preference for gambling only on certainties. But they also possessed a native spirit of enterprise, a readiness to trying anything once, which gave them the edge always on the too-conservative and cynical English.

One of the most successful and typical Scots of this present age was a Glasgow draper named Hugh Fraser. To the end he would arrive at the shop early in the morning and greet women customers by name, but meanwhile he bought up a number of stores in Scotland and the English provinces and many of the largest in London, including that holy of holies called Harrods. He worked hard at the same time to create winter sports resorts in the Scottish Highlands, and he ended several times a pound millionaire and, of course, a Lord. (Moreover, like many Scottish successful men, he left behind a son who was able to continue the good work.)

The Scots have also been great newspapermen in modern times, but primarily as proprietors and editors. America's first newspaper, *The Boston News-Letter,* was founded in 1704 by John Campbell of the hated clan; and much of the credit for modern press methods must be assigned to that James Gordon Bennett whose folk came from Scotland. He sent Stanley to find Livingstone (another Scot), and it was his work on the old *New York Herald* particularly which established many of the patterns of modern journalism. The first of the private eyes was Allan Pinkerton, from Glasgow.

Voltaire said that the best human achievement was that of the gardener who concentrated on cultivation of plants when others were more interested in destruction. And the Scottish talent for financial improvement might be linked with their equal skill as horticulturalists. Some of the best, if necessarily the worst-tempered gardeners in the world, both professionals and amateurs, have been Scotsmen. A typical product is the lovely Golden Gate Park, San Francisco, as created by John McLaren.

Politicians are left to the last. This can be their privilege or the opposite, according to taste. What the Scots have produced is a remarkable number of highly successful human manipulators *of the second class* in all the English-speaking countries. And they have contributed to the blood of one or two really eminent world statesmen.

Once again the process began with the Act of Union. Only when she became linked to England did Scotland throw up the really successful men. The first was that Earl of Bute who became the original Scots Prime Minister of Great Britain thanks to pandering to the desire of King George III to rule as a person and not a puppet. He broke the power of the Whigs and more or less established the Tory Party, but his policies led to ignominy and disaster and the eventual loss of the American colonies—and to the popularity of a much greater man, William Pitt. Bute was not liked and he was laughed at, the fates of all too many Scottish rulers of England.

More than half of the American Presidents have had some Scottish blood (including, the Roosevelts and Lyndon B. Johnson). John Witherspoon, founder of Princeton, signed the Declaration of Independence together with another Scot, James Wilson. (And, while we are on this subject of Scottish blood in famous men, let it be noted that John D. Rockefeller possessed some, and also Charles de Gaulle.)

But, the British Prime Ministers! William Ewart Gladstone was born like the Beatles in Liverpool, the son of a rich merchant, and educated at Eton, and entered Parliament as a Tory. As a typical descendant of Aberdonians he changed his coat when it became necessary and made his name as a Liberal Prime Minister, the first to govern Britain from what we now regard as the Left. He introduced elementary education for the working classes, and vote by ballot. He tried to give Ireland at least Home Rule but failed (as all have failed with Ireland). He was a high-living, strait-laced, formidable and very religious man, one of whose hobbies was the reform of prostitutes. If any man was a Great Victorian it was William Ewart Gladstone. He was succeeded as British Prime Minister by another Scot, Archibald Philip Primrose, fifth Earl of Rosebery. He had been highly successful in less important offices, but failed as the man in charge and fell in a year, after which he turned his coat back from Liberal to high Tory. In his old age he achieved real British fame not so much from his various, pompously written books on great men as from his winning of that horse-racing classic the Derby. (At that period people achieved the same lustre from racehorse ownership as teenagers achieve from singing crude songs on television today.)

Arthur James Balfour was the son of a Scottish landowner, and became Tory Prime Minister of Britain in 1902. He suffered a crushing defeat at the elections of 1905 over the issue of "tariff reform," but came back to minor power as a member of the Government during the First World War. It was this Scotsman who issued the Balfour Declaration, 1917, in favor of a national home in Palestine for the Jews, and he will doubtless be remembered more for that than for his several books on philosophy. He knew as a Scot what it was to be persecuted as one of a peculiar people.

Meanwhile James Keir Hardie of Lanarkshire had been the first Labor candidate to stand for Parliament and was the founder of the

British Independent Labor Party. Also he was a pioneer pacifist—in the Boer War.

Henry Campbell-Bannerman was a Glasgow man who, as Liberal leader, inflicted that crushing defeat on Balfour in 1905. He was one of the first to give self-government to African colonies and to bestow upon the trades unions that measure of power which was eventually almost to wreck the country. Fortunately he had to resign in 1908 before he could do much more damage and died soon after.

Andrew Bonar Law was a Canadian-Scotsman who returned to his fathers' land to make a fortune there as a banker and ironmaster, then entered the British Parliament and eventually became leader of the Tory opposition to Campbell-Bannerman. He was Prime Minister in 1922 but had to resign from health reasons; and he died the following year.

Ramsay MacDonald from Lossiemouth has already had his share in this book, but must be mentioned here as Britain's first Labor Prime Minister (in 1924) and finally the failure who was broken not only by the 1932 economic crisis but also by his vanity and susceptibility to the fleshpots of a still-capitalist world.

Although Harold Macmillan was a wealthy publisher and was educated as a typical member of the English establishment at Eton and Oxford, he was the descendant of a family of crofters in the Western Isles of Scotland, one of whom came to London as a bookseller. Macmillan succeeded Eden as Prime Minister in 1957. He was the most successful of political leaders for a while, giving the country what it wanted in the way of more and more money from the printing presses and in the way of returning to native peoples what had once been the British Empire. Then he fell most spectacularly because a subordinate had been consorting with prostitutes and spies (and because England had suddenly developed its first, properly-satirical television program).

He was, of course, succeeded by another Scot, the fourteenth Earl of Home, who renounced the title so that he could work from the House of Commons as Sir Alec Douglas-Home. He was for a while excellent, witty and lively, and might have continued as Prime Minister for a long time but for two circumstances. The first was Britain's realization that if it must have a government of socialists then perhaps the real socialists might be best. The second was Home's image as a be-gaitered and grouse-shooting aristocrat in an age of blue jeans. This was a sufficiently ironic development, considering the impoverished and coarse history of the Scots.

Home became Foreign Secretary in the eventual Heath Government, but remained a little too upper-class for the highest office.

The British Dominions overseas all suffered a talkative succession of Scottish heads of state, or at least heads of state with Scottish blood, right down to that Canadian Premier Pierre Elliott Trudeau (who has been known on certain evening occasions to wear a kilt of the Elliott tartan).

Scottish achievements in international sport could be mentioned if a half-Scottish writer did not want to appear too boastful, but perhaps it should be pointed out that a world motor racing champion is a Scot, Jackie Stewart, and that Neil Armstrong, of Caledonian descent, was after all the first man on the moon.

One of the most typical Scots of all was Samuel Smiles, who wrote *Self Help*.

12

EXPLANATION

A S all human beings are queer when observed with a candid eye,
no matter their superficial sameness of clothes and manners,
so are all countries if the observer takes the trouble to look beneath
the skin for divergencies from the norm.

From the Middle West this Scotland might appear just a romantic
old country with kilts and bagpipes and a proud history, but of course
it is much more than that.

To begin with, what is wrong with it that it has not achieved the
success of others?

Greece is similarly a hard, small land with a lack of mineral resources, but there was a time when it conquered all its neighbors, and
its ideas and arts have profoundly influenced the course of human
progress. Scotland as a nation has never succeeded in war comparably, and her contribution of the tartan to the world's arts can by no
stretch of the imagination be regarded as important. Neither Platonic
virtues nor Solonic reforms have comparably come from Scotland,
which has contributed no ideological terms to the language of ideas
such as democracy, logic, ethics, physics, even oligarchy.

Perhaps Switzerland has a more similar background to Scotland
than Greece. Her people originally came from the same "Celtic"
stock. But Switzerland successfully and permanently resisted her
neighbors in war and finally became a civic model for others, a
country that taught the world how to keep out of strife.

Poor Scotland proved incapable of protecting herself and ended as
part of England. She gave the world no men of supreme genius in
intellect, the arts or politics, unless that writer of vernacular songs,
Robert Burns, were to be taken erroneously at the face value which
Scottish patriots naturally place upon him.

Maybe it depends upon how you look at it. Perhaps Scotland contributed as much with the steam engine as Greece with the idea of democracy. Maybe her doctors did even more for humanity than the neutralist legislators of Switzerland. And, if she failed to resist England at least she had the sense to combine with that country and thus be responsible for a great part of what nineteenth and early twentieth century Britain did for the world.

But a truly patriotic Scotsman, when he returns to his country after experiences in greater, more successful lands, must inevitably feel the sadness of inferiority. Why?

Scotland consists of its physical territory and its people. The territory as such could be worse. The greater part is barren mountains but there are at least as many fertile valleys as Greece and Switzerland possess. Moreover Scotland enjoys natural resources which those others lack, notably in coal and fish.

But in one very important respect Scotland is physically inferior to most similar countries, and that is in climate. Most of the great Greek ideas came naturally from her sunshine and mild sea breezes. The philosophers were men who sat in the open air under trees, drinking wine. They were encouraged thus to think fruitfully. Similarly Switzerland has an infinitely more helpful climate than Scotland, very cold and dry in the winter, happily warm for the rest of the year.

Scotland's climate has never been temperate enough to produce that ease of mind which suddenly erupts in the world-shattering ideas, nor has it been hard enough, such as that of Scandinavia and Russia, to transform men into ravening wild beasts, like the Viking and other hordes.

It is cold in the winter but, throughout the year, is moistly affected by western winds from across the Atlantic. There is always too much damp air, without the compensating warmth that often helps England. It is not, however, quite so humid as Ireland.

The strange Irish climate is such as to dissuade men both from lying about and generating great art and philosophies, and from taking brisk steps to improve their environment. At least the Scottish climate has encouraged handiwork. The people have always worked in a kind of fury to make a better world *physically*. Fine houses have been built, and ships, and finally engines. Diseases have been tackled and cured. Overseas territories have not been conquered by Scotland as such but they have been consistently colonized and made better in the physical sense by Scotsmen. When a soft rain is continually falling from the warm west and is blown about by piercingly cold winds from the east, then it is difficult to create immortal art or propound world-shaking ideas. But one is stimulated to build a strong house quickly and to construct better devices for everyday living, right down to the mackintosh and to television.

Being thus constructed climatically Scotland did not get the best people when the original migrations of modern man occurred. She was right at the end of the road, and there was not even a road in those days of defective communications. Not for nothing did the ancients find Ultima Thule at the top of Scotland. It was for them like deep space beyond the galaxies is to explorers in the second half of the twentieth century.

Perhaps Scotland got the most *enterprising* people. They were those who were wiling to push the frontier out to its final edge. But the best people in the material sense were those who acquired and could hold the most fertile lands with the most salubrious climates. The "Celts" or their even more mysterious predecessors swarmed over the wonderful land which we now know as France. They crossed to the southern part of what is now England and took the best places there. Even Wales was not so bad. But those who failed to hold good land in the south of the British Isles had to push on north. At least they were relatively safe up there. The strong people would not bother about them, as nothing they possessed could be worth having.

And so it was all through the history of this land, right up to the present day. Refugees in recent times such as the Jews, Poles, Hungarians, Negroes and Indians have naturally tried to get settled in southern England rather than in bleak, comparatively impoverished Scotland. London is crowded with such enterprising people but not Edinburgh and certainly not Aberdeen.

When the ancient Romans came they efficiently pushed right up to Scotland but shivered and left only unhappy garrisons there. They did not bother to *civilize* Scotland as they civilized England (anymore than they had either the equipment or desire to civilize what we now call Germany). Thus Scotland lacked the fertilizing touch of Greece through Rome in the early days—and similarly never got what the Vikings gave to much of Europe. When the longboats ground ashore on the coasts of Normandy their rufous crews wondered at the lushness of the land and naturally stayed. The Vikings who came to Scotland were those who lost those more golden opportunities: not the very best of the Vikings. As it was with other peoples afterwards. Scotland was the California of that early migration period without the sun and the natural resources: and the best settlers of America were not those who finally came to the Pacific seaboard.

On the other hand the men who reached California were pretty tough, and so were those who penetrated into and stayed in the bleak wilderness of remote Scotland. That toughness was transmitted to their descendants and modified by the climate and other aspects of living conditions. The Scots became what we know them as now, strong, enterprising, kind-hearted, class-conscious but only in an inverted way. ("I'm as good a man as he is even if he lives in a bloody castle.")

Those of them who survived the climate, a climate particularly productive of respiratory diseases, became strong enough to master the physical handicaps of their land. They became inventive and hard-working but never thoughtful in the high, philosophic sense. Most of their thinking went either into gadgetry as necessitated by the harsh environment, or else into a kind of religion.

The students of comparative religion say theology started when men got tired of natural disasters and wondered if there were not powers in the universe that needed placating. The worst early religions were those that never advanced beyond this primitive stage, as the best were those which eventually concentrated upon defects in human nature that could perhaps be cured by training.

The Scots had such a difficult life in their Ultima Thule that they embraced the primitive kind of religion from the first and never let go. Their churches knew nothing of true spirituality and even less of practical ethics. It was the outward form and not the innermost meaning that took their undivided attention. They became progressively litigious, fractious, schismatic and, from the Christian point of view in particular, completely unChristian. This was one of the factors that inhibited their invention of world-shattering ideas rather than steam engines. Possibly similar factors can be seen at work in modern America, which was originally in considerable part a Scottish colony.

So they started in an inhospitable land which nobody else wanted and they were people who had been forced up there because "better" people had taken the more fructifying lands.

And in due course they naturally developed that inferiority complex and became jealous of the only neighbors they had, those English who had taken and held the better lands to the south. Thus the fatal love-hate marriage between Scotland and England was eventually solemnized and originally based.

It started when the first wild chieftain said to his followers: "They've got fat cattle and soft women down there. Let's make a raid."

For hundreds of years the Scots periodically rode down across the border, like Indians in the Wild West, and set fire to peaceful villages, pillaged and raped. And for hundreds of years the English had to respond with stern punitive expeditions.

As a result the tourist today is advised, as in an early chapter of this book, to wander from the beaten track into the great open spaces of the world's most spectacular border country, that between Scotland and England. It is enormously wide, a record-sized no man's land compared with that between most other countries. It is relatively unspoilt, to use a word that has become pejorative but still has no synonym.

The fact that the Scots lost to the English in the final battles could be charitably ascrbied to their always inferior numbers and resources. But the Swiss were similarly outnumbered by the Austrians, the French, the Germans and the Italians, and fought them back one by one and kept their independence at the point of the sword.

The Scots did not thus prevail because, unlike the Swiss, they could never keep together a united army for long. They quarreled together and the chieftains took offense and was each one of them a sulky Ulysses in his tent eventually. Others, being descendants of those deprived people forced to the world's rim, were too apt to accept English bribes and become traitors to the idea of Scotland as such. There was a definite defect in what we call "patriotism" here. It is obvious that if leading Israelis today behaved like the Campbells and others in Scotland and worked for the Egyptians and Russians secretly, then there would not be much chance of lasting independence for Israel.

Those fatal Stuarts represented the ultimate in Scottishness. Soft words should not be used to describe them. They were utterly unreliable and sold their country down the creek. Like the first Scottish Labor Prime Minister of England later they preferred the fleshpots of London to those of their native land, and the ultimate union between the two countries was the product of their greed.

Similarly the success of the Union—and it was and always has been a great success—proceeded from the desire of a majority of Scottish people to participate in the profits of England. Those profits meant more than the idea of Scotland as such. It is, of course, only when he turns away from short-term gains that a man retains his soul. That is the true meaning of the misinterpreted fulminations of the Jewish agitator Christ against rich men who did not know the right way to enter the kingdom of heaven. That agitator was not against money as such. He advised his followers to render to Caesar that which was Caesar's, and he tried not unsuccessfully to multiply not only loaves but also fishes. What Christ meant was that you got a better price ultimately if you did not accept the first offer.

The Scots were interested only in getting England's money. They would, like Switzerland, have got much more money in the long run if they had preserved their national sense of independence at all costs and made themselves, as they could have been, the bankers of the world.

In London they became such bankers, and in France, and in America and the British dominions overseas. But their own country was weakened by each service they performed for the conquering English and for other foreigners.

This, of course, is written only from the viewpoint of a nationalist political philosophy. But that is the philosophy of a world which, for the time being, is made that way. And Scotland is not a proud, independent country, and she has strangely failed to attain the heights of others that originally had fewer advantages; and it has been necessary to reason why.

Let us finally insist upon what remains good. Much has been said about the bad features of Scotland because a real effort has been made to explain why such a beautiful country of clever and pugnacious people has failed so palpably to attain the heights. It has been possible to make this effort because the human mind, for all its faults, has become increasingly more self-critical. A glory of the twentieth century is this ability to take a cool new look at ancient, worn-out shibboleths. In the nineteenth century it was the official view that all was really for the best in the best possible of worlds. Then the accepted ideas and the great nations tumbled, and we came down to a kind of moral and artistic and intellectual anarchy. But at least we were given our first chance in hundreds of years to query why without fear of prison, banishment or obloquy.

The best features of Scotland are her purpled hills and chatter streams, her rural and her fishing communities, her high courage in single combat, and her enormous skill in the practical application of science and in colonization of other lands.

Only England has been her equal as a colonist, and a close examination of the situation might reveal that England would never have developed an empire at all if it had not been for the Scotsmen who acted as the spearhead of her thrusts.

The Dutch originally mapped most of the new lands but did not develop the same worldwide empire as the British because they had no Scots to do the permanent dirty work. Without the aid of those chameleon-like, earnest men from the north England might just have gone as far as the Dutch, the Germans, the Latins overseas but no farther. Those were people who took territories from natives and left behind forts and trading posts. Semi-permanent, really successful colonization took place only when there were Scots to adapt themselves to strange conditions and work hard and stay there permanently. They were out to make money principally and they succeeded but meanwhile they brought immeasurable benefits to the natives, roads, dams, bridges, schools, medical services and organization both for war and peace.

The Scots gushed out from their bleak little country like worker ants upon the world, and that inevitably enervated the bleak little country.

No accurate estimate has been made of the number of Scots who fell in the two world wars, but it must have comprised a considerable part of the male issue of two generations. Add to these the enterprising men who went to the United States, Canada, Australia, South Africa, New Zealand, many African colonies and to India, Malaysia, China, even Europe, and it will be appreciated how the strength of a small country was dissipated or disseminated.

It is true that England and Germany and France lost even more men in the wars, and maybe to colonization also, but from much larger populations.

Does it ring true and does it convince? Of course not. Scotland, unfortunately, had lost its soul and failed to attain its ambitions long before the modern wars and emigrations.

All the same a world balance sheet would contain a considerable item of credit, headed "Scottish Contribution to Pioneering Work in Overseas Lands and to Freedom Wars." What would the world have benefitted the most from, a Scottish Einstein or Rembrandt or Shakespeare, or that remarkable everyday work done in jungle and prairie and in the forefront always of the armies which have defeated tyrants everywhere and left behind them not burning cities but good public services where there were none before?

Then there is no doubt at all that few people have given so many practical inventions to the world as the Scots. Without this genius we might have had to wait a little bit longer (perhaps much longer) for such as the steam engine, the steamboat, the telephone and phonograph, modern methods of roadmaking, the bicycle, the pneumatic tire, even television, radar and the mackintosh.

Without the work of Scottish medical scientists thousands, for some considerable time longer, would have continued to die from many loathsome diseases or would have continued to suffer excruciating pain under the surgeon's unclean knife. And the tropics would have remained fevered and uninhabitable to the white man.

Half of America's presidents would have been quite different men without the Scottish blood in them, and what Britain would have done for Prime Ministers is nobody's business. As the most useful men on a committee are those of the second-rate, so the cabinets and government departments would have languished without their steady stiffening of worthy and hard-working if rarely really eminent Scots.

Scotland, as a small country, has already been compared rather disadvantageously with Greece and Switzerland, perhaps mainly because of the similar physical character of these lands. Another useful and revelatory comparison could be made with Holland, which has less than half the area but double the population.

No Scotsmen have equalled Rembrandt (and indeed dozens of lesser Dutch artists) nor attained the world influence of a single Erasmus. And, whereas Scotland could never make the supreme effort to cast off the conquering English, Holland successfully drove out an even more overwhelming predator, the cruelly-imperial Spain (out of which success her great art emerged as from a crucible of fire).

But the Scots have given humanity many more useful machines than the Dutch and have cured or assuaged more of mankind's ills; and as settlers in new lands and fighters against modern tyrants they have a record that is nicer by comparison. Should a primitive people be asked to choose between a Scotsman and a Dutchman for either a new master or a protector there can be no doubt of the answer. The Scots might have many faults but these have gained them only friends. They possess the almost unique distinction of being universally liked because their coronets have always been accompanied by kind hearts and because, above all, they have never lost that "common touch" which in the modern world is the most favored of everyday attributes.

This people compare, indeed, only with the Jews as universal men. Similarly they have done more for other nations everywhere than they have done for their own, and they have been curiously adaptable in the same way. They have shared a skill in finance and organization, but the Scots have not attained the artistic heights as have the Jews and really cannot match them upon the upper levels of intellectual subtlety. But the peoples are very, very similar and might even have been related in some remote past.

There is above all a sameness in their sad songs; and the visitor to Scotland who enjoys most the characteristic Caledonian manifestations of song and dance, pipes and tartan, will understand these better if told that they are essentially efforts to compensate for a profound inferiority complex.

Big, successful nations do not need the boasts of little, failed ones. The unhappiness of essential non-success produces not only the calypsos of the Caribbean and the jazz of New Orleans and the sorrowful laments of the Psalmist—"By the waters of Babylon I sat down and wept"—but also the strangely-accented way of speaking of the Scots, and their falsified kilts and their Aberdonian jokes about meanness, and even their over-worship of such national figures as Bruce and Burns. These distinctly Scottish characteristics make the place interesting to the tourist, but they are also the protective coloring of sensitive souls who need that kind of help.

All the same there is nothing quite like Scotland anywhere else. A visit there will be more rewarding than to many sunnier places, and the people encountered will always be remembered as less inhuman than any in the wide world.

INDEX